P9-DGV-330

LOST *and* FOUND

ALSO BY GENEEN ROTH

Women Food and God

The Craggy Hole in My Heart and the Cat Who Fixed It

Breaking Free from Emotional Eating

When You Eat at the Refrigerator, Pull Up a Chair

Appetites

Feeding the Hungry Heart

When Food Is Love

Why Weight?

LOST *and* FOUND

Unexpected Revelations *About* FOOD and MONEY

· GENEEN ROTH ·

VIKING

VIKING
Published by the
Penguin Group
Penguin Group (USA) Inc., 375 Hudson Street, New York, New York 10014, U.S.A.
Penguin Group (Canada), 90 Eglinton Avenue East, Suite 700, Toronto, Ontario,
Canada M4P 2Y3 (a division of Pearson Penguin Canada Inc.)
Penguin Books Ltd, 80 Strand, London WC2R 0RL, England
Penguin Ireland, 25 St. Stephen's Green, Dublin 2, Ireland (a division of Penguin Books Ltd)
Penguin Books Australia Ltd, 250 Camberwell Road, Camberwell, Victoria 3124,
Australia (a division of Pearson Australia Group Pty Ltd)
Penguin Books India Pvt Ltd, 11 Community Centre, Panchsheel Park, New Delhi – 110 017, India
Penguin Group (NZ), 67 Apollo Drive, Rosedale, North Shore 0632, New Zealand
(a division of Pearson New Zealand Ltd)
Penguin Books (South Africa) (Pty) Ltd, 24 Sturdee Avenue, Rosebank, Johannesburg 2196, South Africa

Penguin Books Ltd, Registered Offices:
80 Strand, London WC2R 0RL, England

First published in 2011 by Viking Penguin,
a member of Penguin Group (USA) Inc.

1 3 5 7 9 10 8 6 4 2

Grateful acknowledgment is made for permission to reprint the following copyrighted works:
Selection from *Falling into Grace* by Adyashanti. © 2010 Adyashanti. Reprinted by permission of the publisher, Sounds True. "Kindness" from *Words Under the Words: Selected Poems* by Naomi Shihab Nye. Copyright © 1995 by Naomi Shihab Nye. Reprinted by permission of Far Corner Books, Portland, Oregon. Selection from *The Essential Rumi,* translations by Coleman Barks with John Moyne (HarperCollins). Copyright © 1995 by Coleman Barks. Reprinted by permission of Coleman Barks.

LIBRARY OF CONGRESS CATALOGING IN PUBLICATION DATA
Roth, Geneen.
Lost and found : unexpected revelations about food and money / Geneen Roth.
p. cm.
Includes index.
ISBN 978-0-670-02271-7 (hardback)
1. Finance, Personal—Psychological aspects. 2. Money—Psychological aspects.
3. Food habits—Psychological aspects. I. Title.
HG179.R6915 2011
332.024—dc22 2010048242

Printed in the United States of America
Set in Perpetua
Designed by Kate Nichols

To Matt and Celeste, for always finding me

CONTENTS

LOST *and* FOUND

PROLOGUE

What Was Lost

I was standing in my kitchen wondering what to have for lunch when my friend Taj called.

"Sit down," she said.

I thought she was going to tell me she had just gotten the haircut from hell. I laughed and said, "It can't be that bad."

But it was. Before the phone call I had thirty years of retirement savings in a "safe" fund with a brilliant financial guru. When I put down the phone, my savings were gone and my genius financial guru, Bernie Madoff, was in handcuffs. I felt as if I had died and, for some unknown reason, was still breathing.

Since Madoff's arrest on charges of running a sixty-five-billion-dollar Ponzi scheme, I've read many articles about how we Madoff investors should have known what was going on, how believing in Madoff was no different from believing there were WMD in Iraq. And I wish I could say I had reservations about Madoff before "the Call." I wish I could say I knew better about getting such consistently good returns, but I did not. Besides, everything I "knew better" about—stocks, smart financial advisers, real estate—had also proved disastrous: Our financial adviser embezzled a quarter of our money years ago, I lost another third in the stock market during the boom times, and we bought our house at the top of the market and sold at the bottom. Considering that, Madoff seemed like a respite—his fund showed occasional losses along with small, steady gains. (I'm keeping a list of people who want to be notified of our next investment so they can sprint in the other direction. Feel free to add your name.)

• • • • •

It was always more important for me to find work that I loved than to be rich. I know this is an attitude that reflects enormous privilege, since so much of the world lives on less than a dollar a day and must concern itself with getting food. But I was (and still am) unspeakably fortunate: I've always had clean water, sweaters to spare, more than enough to eat.

Although my parents were so poor when they married that they ran out of food money each week by Saturday night, my father worked his way up the corporate ladder—and by the time I was fifteen, our main metric of worth, both in the community and with one another, was our collection of new, shiny things. Cars, shoes, popular people. But like many baby boomers, I spent my college years protesting the Vietnam War, rejecting consumerism and various other activities (like hiring a plastic surgeon to break my nose so that it could look like everyone else's) for the many iterations of "finding myself": therapy, living in India, and meditation. In my late twenties, I spent a year washing dishes and being a maid at a local inn and two years as an avocado-and-cheese sandwich maker in a health-food store so that I could spend early mornings writing. After that, I started my first groups for compulsive eaters in my friends Harry and Sue's house; since I was working as a nanny and living in the bedroom next to their two-year-old daughter, they gave me the use of their living room to begin what seemed like a far-fetched idea: meeting with women like me to explore our relationships to food and weight.

Was I able to reject the pursuit of shiny things because I knew that if I ran out of money or luck, my father could rescue me? I don't know because I don't know what it would have been like to grow up in any other family. What I do know is that I saw what money cost: parents who were cruel to each other; addiction to alcohol and drugs; infidelity; physical and sexual abuse; and self-loathing all around. It was impossible to know if the pursuit of more *caused* the wretchedness, but the connection between misery and money was scalded in my brain—as well as the need to find out if there was more to being alive than being rich and sleeping with your best friend's wife or husband.

. . . . .

During the first year I learned to meditate, my Buddhist teachers took our class to graveyards so we would viscerally understand that we would end up exactly like the people in the ground: dead, very dead. After those excursions, I'd wake up every day and ask myself what I would regret not doing if I died that day, that week, that year. The answers were always the same: figure out the meaning of life (if there was one) and find out why I was here. And write, always write. Making more than enough money wasn't ever part of the mix.

Eventually, after a few years of teaching groups about compulsive eating and having my book proposal rejected by twenty-five publishers, an editor at Bobbs-Merrill accepted my first book. I spent the next ten years teaching workshops and writing more books, doing well enough financially to rent an apartment, drive a used Volvo, and buy as much chocolate as I wanted. In 1992, my fourth book sold enough copies in paperback to spend two weeks on the *New York Times* best-seller list, and when I received the check for this windfall—$106,000—it was like getting a paper bag filled with Monopoly money. I had no idea what to do with it, no way of relating to the fact that I was now one of the ones with money that I didn't like, didn't trust. Or, as James Grant, editor of *Grant's Interest Rate Observer*, says, "Insofar as there is a lesson in history, it's that human beings are not good with large sums of money, anything over $136."

Up to that moment, I had had the luxury of not paying

much attention to money, partly because I was making enough to pay my bills, after which I'd put what was left over in a savings account, and partly because I had met and married my partner, Matt, and I relegated the money part of our lives to him. He made more money than I—enough to put a down payment on a small house in Berkeley—and I assumed that people who could afford to buy a house knew what they were doing in the financial arena. Not only did I feel money dumb, but I also felt that focusing on money—either on ways to make more of it or on how and where to invest it—was complicated, shallow, and spiritually bankrupt. Although I wasn't aware of this until recently, I didn't believe that it was possible to be interested in consciousness and interested in money, to care about deforestation and care about money. I believed that any kind of awakening from what my teachers called samsara, or the delusion of conditioned reality, needed to be separate from money, as if money were as deadly as the plague and even thinking about it would lead me to being one of the bad guys. So I kept making choices based on my unconscious beliefs, and since those beliefs lumped being an aspirant of the contemplative life with remaining ignorant about money, I chose ignorance again and again. Since I couldn't admit that I was making money and was, therefore, like all the moneyed people who I was convinced had no integrity, I just stopped thinking about it. And I stopped taking any responsibility for having it or deciding what to do about it.

When our sweet and very rich friend Richard told us

about a man named Bernie Madoff, with whom he and his family had been successfully invested for many years, we both assumed that Richard was brilliant (otherwise, how had he gotten so rich?) and that investing with Madoff through Richard's family fund was simple, smart, and safe. So within a few years, we turned all our money—nearly a million dollars—over to Madoff. By giving someone else full responsibility for my money, my untarnished self-image could remain intact; I didn't have to think about money or what to do with it: I had Richard, and Richard had Madoff.

Did I hear that diversification was smart? Absolutely. Did I choose to ignore that advice because I also got conflicting advice about Madoff being, as someone said, "the Jewish equivalent of T-bills"? Yes. I chose to find very smart people who (I thought) were as smart in their fields as I was in mine, and I chose to listen to them

Since the Call, I have chanted the mantra of *How could you, why did you, what's the matter with you?* Another, even meaner version of this is *It serves you right. You thought you were above it all, different from everyone else. Well, guess what, honey? You're not.* I have also been eager to blame someone else—anyone else—for the mess. Richard; my accountant, who encouraged me to put all my money in one place; my friends, who all did the same thing. Where does the blame end? My father valued the accumulation of wealth. He said it didn't matter how I did it. But this was after forty members of his family were killed in Auschwitz and his motto became "God abandoned us. There is no such thing as morality, and it's every man for himself." Do I blame my father, who has been dead for eight years? Or is it Hitler's fault that I put my money into a Ponzi scheme?

. . . . .

Unlike many people who lost everything with Madoff, and unlike so much of the world, I still have money to live day to day. I am still teaching, and I am still writing, and there is still nothing else I would rather do. But still. For weeks after the phone call, I went to sleep at night oscillating between ranting about Madoff and being terrified that we wouldn't be able to keep our house. Then I realized that, for me, the real suffering was not living without money; it was living with this ranting mind. The financial and emotional devastation was horrible, but if I didn't allow myself to actually feel it—rather than react to it by blaming myself or someone else—then I couldn't learn what there was to learn. I wouldn't see, for instance, that I had participated in the fraud by being willing to close my eyes about what Madoff was doing. Or that I had pretended not to care about having money or where it was invested. Or the fact that I had been unconscious about money and had kept choosing to stay that way.

During the years we were invested with Madoff, I often asked Richard, the head of our feeder fund, how Madoff made such consistently good returns. Although Richard tried to explain it to me, it was clear he didn't know either, because I'd leave our meetings still unable to explain to anyone else how it worked. But that didn't deter me. And so, rather than put my money where my values were—into real things, real people, real companies—I allowed myself to be part of this insane leveraging of money upon money. I allowed myself to be sucked into the belief that as long as I was donating money to charities, as long as I was doing good work in the world, it was fine to participate in a venture that was not contributing to anything in which I believed. I engaged in the money split to which we as a culture subscribe: We say we believe in wind energy, but we put our money into oil. We say we believe in education and health care, but we put our money into advanced weaponry. We say we want to stop violence, but we allow genocide in Darfur. Over and over again, I've asked myself: *Why didn't I secure the most basic of all things—shelter itself? Why didn't I pay off my mortgage?* And if I don't engage in blame, I see the answer clearly: because I believed in something else more—I believed in remaining unconscious. And I believed in accumulating. And when you believe in accumulating, you see what you don't have, not what you do have.

My relationship to money was no different from my relationship to food, to love, to fabulous sweaters: Because I was never aware of what I already had, I never felt as if I had enough. I was always focused on the bite that was yet to come, not the one in my mouth. I was focused on the way my husband wasn't perfect, not the way he was. And on the jacket I saw in the window, not the one in my closet that I hadn't worn for a year.

In thirty years of exploring compulsive eating, I kept learning that it wasn't about how much or how little I had on my plate or in my mouth. It wasn't about how fattening pizza was or how many calories I burned during my aerobics workout. It wasn't about the glycemic index or Weight Watchers points or the speed of my metabolism. The thing I kept seeing, the thing that changed everything, was that my problems with food weren't about food. They weren't about anything—not anything—out there. The problem was me. My mind, my beliefs, my conflicts, and how I expressed them in everything I did, particularly with the food on my plate and the size of my thighs. It was as if I walked through life as a hungry ghost—with, as the Buddhists say, "a mouth the size of a needle's eye and a stomach the size of a mountain." No matter how much I ate or had or experienced, it didn't satisfy me because I wasn't really taking it in, wasn't absorbing it, wasn't noticing or appreciating it. I always wanted more.

I never applied what I learned about food to money because it seemed as if it didn't apply. Also, I was lazy. I didn't want to work as hard with money as I did with food. I didn't want yet another area of my life about which I needed to take responsibility and be aware. And money seemed to be concrete in a way that food wasn't. Money seemed to be about survival in a way that food wasn't. Money seemed to have certain rules—"Make more than you spend," "Work hard and you'll get far," "Rich people are special"—that seemed unbendable, irrevocable. Problems with money really did seem to be "out there." And even though I could name a parallel food rule I didn't believe for every money rule I did—"Fat makes you fat," "Don't eat after 7:00 P.M. or you'll gain weight," "Thin people are better than me"—I believed that money was *real* in a way that food wasn't. Money was outside of me in a way that food wasn't. Money needed to be handled on the external, not the internal, level in a way that food didn't.

But after we lost our money, I saw that everything I was telling myself about money was just an excuse for me to continue being lazy, compulsive, and unconscious. I saw that there wasn't a huge difference between problems with money and problems with food: Most of the world doesn't have enough of either, but those of us who do seem to always want more and, for the most part, refuse to believe that the problems we are experiencing "out there" originate—and need to first be solved—"in here." With our minds. Our conditioned patterns. Our old ways of believing and feeling and behaving.

Although I never would have chosen the path of losing our life savings, it is forcing me, in the way that my suffering around food forced me, to wake up, pay attention, question the automatic and reactive trance in which I usually live. When I wander into blame or fear (What if my husband or I get sick and we can't pay the medical bills? What if there is an accident and we can't work? What will we do when we get old?), I live in a hell created by my own mind. On this side of the loss, there is the necessity—the urgency—of staying in the moment. This breath. This step. This splash of sun. On the other side of loss, it seems that something priceless still remains.

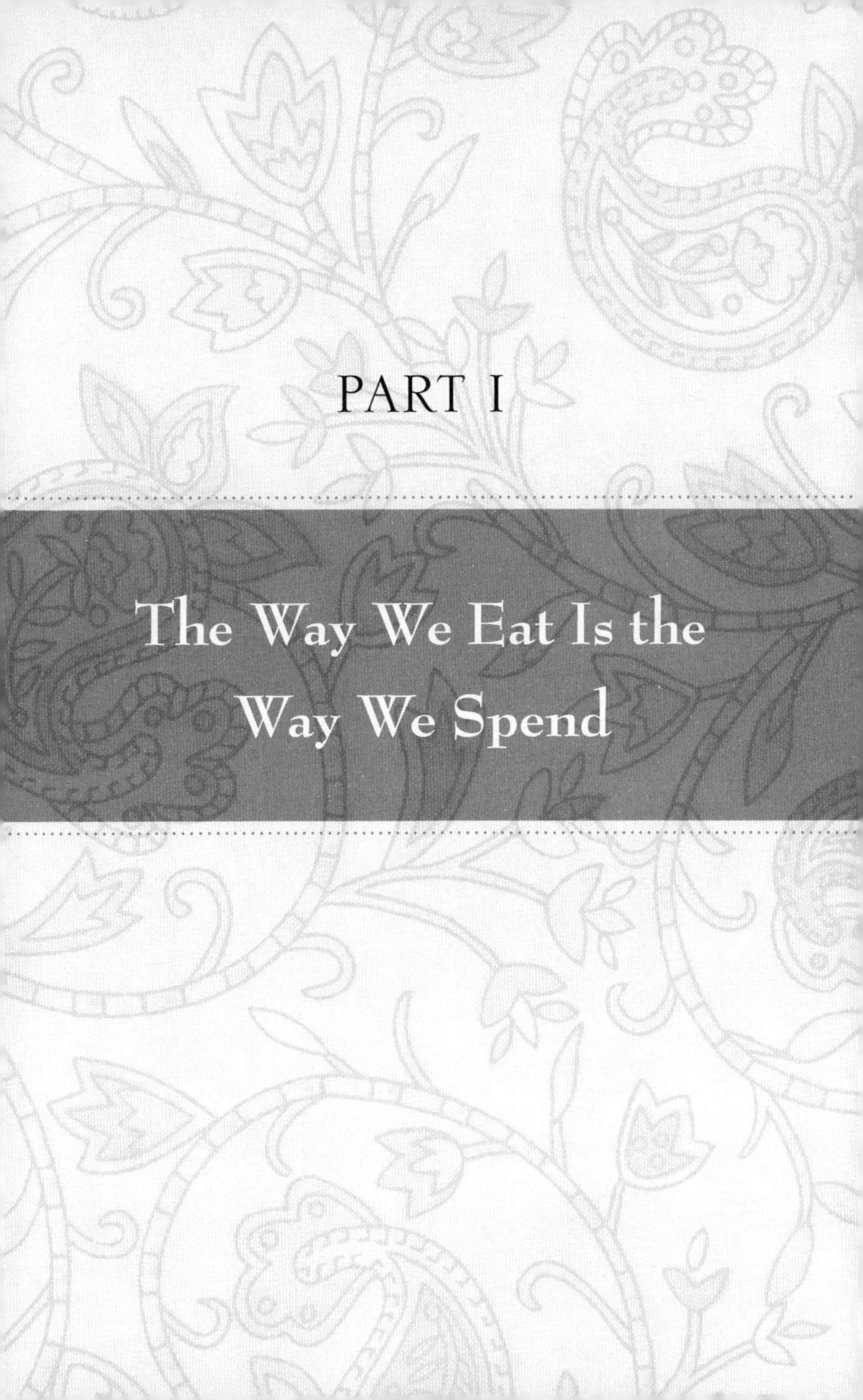

PART I

The Way We Eat Is the Way We Spend

1

Only Kindness

Twenty minutes after Taj called to tell me that Madoff was a fraud and that our money was gone, I was still sitting on the couch when a stray thought flew by: Matt. I needed to tell my husband. Matt was sailing on a Russian ice-breaker in Antarctica; he'd left a week before to romp with emperor penguins and old college friends and would be gone for two more weeks. I had a piece of paper with instructions about how to get in touch with him, but each of the three oceans he was sailing on had its own area code, and I had no idea where he was at the moment.

In the weeks leading to his departure, I had already been counting the days until he returned. I'd kept telling myself that it was good for us to be apart, that we missed each other when one of us was gone. Also that the chances of a big, terrible thing happening when he was away were minimal: It was only three weeks, and many three-week segments had passed over the years without a disaster happening. I'd flipped through the usual catastrophes: his mother, my mother, car accidents, broken bones, sudden illnesses, nuclear bombs, asteroids colliding with the earth, a deadly strain of bird flu. None of them had included losing thirty years of life savings.

After finding the list of numbers, I took a chance on any old ocean, dialed, and asked to talk to Matt.

Static. Steps. Matt.

"Hello?" He sounded breathless, excited.

"Hi, honey," I said.

"Is something wrong?" he asked.

"No one died," I answered. And then, between the waves of silence and static, I said, "We've lost all our money. Madoff is in handcuffs. All these years, it's been a fraud, a huge Ponzi scheme."

Static. Silence. Static. Then: "Oh my God."

I could hear his friend Robert, who'd also invested with Madoff, in the background. "What?" Robert said. "What is it? What happened?"

"It's Madoff," Matt said. "The money is gone. All of it."

In the space of the oceans between us, Matt managed to say, "We'll be okay, sweetheart. We will. I am not sure how, but we will be fine."

Then Matt said, "Geneen?"

"Yes?"

"We have to get off the phone. We are no longer the kind of people who can afford to talk on ten-dollar-a-minute satellite phones."

We laughed big, hiccuppy, staticky laughs. Then we cried. After that, we hung up. That phone call cost us a hundred dollars of money we no longer had.

Then I called my spiritual teacher Jeanne, with whom I had been working for fourteen years. "Madoff was arrested," I blurted. "We've lost our life savings."

Jeanne was silent. Finally she said, "Are you sure?"

"Yes."

"Geneen?" she said.

I didn't answer.

"I know this is shocking. And you will probably need to spend some time crying and feeling angry and grieving. But I promise you that nothing of any value is lost."

"How can you say that?" I asked with mounting panic. I was thinking to myself that now was definitely not the time to be spiritual. "Thirty years of life savings are gone. We'll never get those years back. We'll have to sell our house, move in with friends. We might be homeless, sick—and all without money."

"I'm saying it because it's true," she said simply. As if reading my mind, she added, "If there ever is a time to remember what you value most, now is that time."

Jeanne had never lied to me in fourteen years. I trusted her more than I trusted anyone on the earth, even Matt. "I believe you," I said, and then added, "sort of." She told me she'd call me later, and we hung up.

I stood in the kitchen for what seemed like five years, a whole century. Not knowing what else to do, I called my friend Catherine and told her what happened. She gasped, "This is terrible. He's a horrible excuse for a human being."

"Yes," I said. "Horrible."

Catherine added, "But everything that matters is still here."

It was maddening to be told that everything was still fine. That nothing of value was lost. That I still had what mattered. I was devastated by grief, frozen with shock. Here it was: the Catastrophe I'd been anticipating for fifty years, the One for which I'd been saving and protecting my money like my mother saved silk blouses. The End of Days had come, and it was now; the problem was that the disaster for which I'd been storing was the very one in which I'd lost what I'd been storing.

And it happened while Matt couldn't get home, which underscored my second-biggest fear: being alone in a disaster and falling apart from the chaos and panic, not being able to tolerate the suffering around me or in my own mind.

I was still standing in the kitchen when Taj called back.

"We're having a meeting tonight at my house. Many Madoff investors we know are coming. Bring something to eat; be here at seven."

"Okay," I muttered, grateful to have someone directing me what to do and where to go now. I didn't know how much time had passed since Taj had first called, but I couldn't figure out why I should move, and my mind seemed to be frozen in place; it seemed as if I could have stood there all night long.

Then I remembered my friend Kim. In September, three months before Madoff confessed, she'd asked me what I thought she should do with the money from the sale of her house in Woodstock. Feeling incredibly wise and unbelievably helpful, I'd told her about Bernie Madoff, while warning her that she shouldn't do anything on my recommendation alone. "I definitely don't think you should put all your money in one place," I'd added, "even though that's exactly what we did."

Kim had met with a colleague of Richard's about joining a similar feeder fund and within two weeks had deposited all the money she had in a new Madoff account. Now it was gone.

"Kim?" I said when she picked up.

"Hi, Geneen. I'm on my way out. Can I call you back later?"

"I think you should hear this now. But it's bad news, so I recommend that you sit down or do whatever you do when you are about to hear bad news."

"With a lead-in like that, I'm glued to the phone. What is it?"

"Taj called. She told me that Madoff is a fraud and all the money—everyone's money—is gone."

"But that's impossible," she sputtered. "I just spoke to Joel [the feeder fund guy] yesterday, and he told me the money made six percent this year."

"That was yesterday. Madoff confessed today to running a Ponzi scheme for the last few decades. He was just arrested."

"But that just can't be true. I have my statement right here."

"I know, I know. I can't believe it either. And I am so sorry for my part in getting you into this mess. Why don't you come over when you're done with whatever it is you were just about to do. We'll talk, and we can go to the Madoff investors' meeting that Taj is organizing tonight. You can spend the night."

"I have no money. That was it, all I had," Kim said. Then, "I'll be there in an hour."

After hanging up the phone, I still couldn't move. I felt as if a bomb had crashed through my chest and left me in pieces, but my body was still intact. A hummingbird whizzed by. Then I thought of a poem that I'd once read by Naomi Shihab Nye called "Kindness." I couldn't recall any of the lines, but I remembered the word *sorrow*, and I remembered something about losing what you saved and that kindness was prominent, was, in this poem, the outcome of devastation.

Kindness.

I said the word to the stove, the walls, the refrigerator. The sound it made, the feeling of it in my mouth, made me want to cry.

Suddenly, I didn't want to do anything but read that poem. I took a step with my right leg; it was stiff. Then I took another step, and another. I opened the back door, walked out to my writing studio, opened the door. There was my desk, with the papers near my computer in the same place I'd left them before I went into the house for lunch. The butter-colored flowers on the carpet were still there; the picture of Matt and me at a party was displayed innocently on my desk. A mug of cold tea was sitting on a beaded white coaster next to my keyboard. How could those things still be here? How could everything, even the walls, look the same when nothing was?

I found the "Kindness" poem.

Before you know what kindness really is
you must lose things,
feel the future dissolve in a moment
like salt in a weakened broth.
What you held in your hand,
what you counted and carefully saved,
all this must go so you know
how desolate the landscape can be
between the regions of kindness.
How you ride and ride
thinking the bus will never stop,
the passengers eating maize and chicken
will stare out the window forever.

Before you learn the tender gravity of kindness
you must travel where the Indian in a white poncho
lies dead by the side of the road.
You must see how this could be you,
how he too was someone

who journeyed through the night with plans
and the simple breath that kept him alive.

Before you know kindness as the deepest thing inside,
You must know sorrow as the other deepest thing.
You must wake up with sorrow.
You must speak to it till your voice
catches the thread of all sorrows
and you see the size of the cloth.

Then it is only kindness that makes sense anymore,
only kindness that ties your shoes
and sends you out into the day to mail letters and purchase
bread,
only kindness that raises its head
from the crowd of the world to say
It is I you have been looking for,
and then goes with you everywhere
like a shadow or a friend.

I wanted to climb into the space between the lines, lose myself in the rhythm of the words. I wanted to believe that Shihab Nye knew for certain that kindness could be found here, in loss. I sat down on the couch, holding the book in my hands, saying the words out loud.

feel the future dissolve in a moment.

In one phone call.

What you held in your hand,
what you counted and carefully saved,
all this must go . . .

The words seemed to tether me to one breath, then prompt another.

Before you know kindness as the deepest thing inside,
You must know sorrow as the other deepest thing.

It was there, in that turn—before you know kindness, you must know sorrow—that I could begin to relax. Because although I knew without a doubt that I'd always wanted kindness—or lovingkindness, as the Buddhists say—to become automatic and that I said I was willing to do anything for that to happen, I also knew that I probably wouldn't get there gracefully, without kicking and screaming. This, it seemed, was the kicking and screaming part.

I once had a Tibetan Buddhist boyfriend who had a teacher named Lama Yeshe. When he—the lama—was dying of heart failure, he said that if he'd waited until he was sick to practice meditation and kindness, it would have been too hard; he was in too much pain. But because he'd spent years practicing when he wasn't in pain, love itself (for himself, for all beings) was automatic. His mind was already grooved by kindness;

the path was well traveled. "Practice now," he told my boyfriend, "so that when it gets hard, you already know the way."

As I was sitting on the couch in my studio, I understood that this moment was (part of) why I'd been practicing all these years. That I'd been meditating and doing inquiry and watching my mind so that when I faced a situation like this, the truth of kindness could burn through the kicking and shoving and have its way with me.

As if from another galaxy, I heard these words: *If this is what it takes to wake up from the trance of I-me-mine, sign me up. I am willing to learn extreme kindness through extreme devastation.* But from the everyday personality place, I also heard, *WHO CARES ABOUT KINDNESS? JUST GIVE ME MY DAMN MONEY BACK.*

I walked to my computer, typed the name Bernie Madoff into Google, and began reading about his arrest.

The doorbell rang. Kim.

She was standing there, in black velvet shirt and jeans, looking dazed and grief-stricken. The first thing she said was, "I need to find that 'Kindness' poem. Do you have it?"

• • • • •

At Taj's that night, about fifteen of us sat in her living room talking in hushed tones about losing our life savings. Since each of us had heard about Madoff from Richard, Taj's ex-husband, we had followed his example by depositing all that we had in our Madoff accounts. Matt and I had five thousand dollars left in our combined checking accounts. Benjamin had six thousand dollars, a wife, a house, and three kids. Moira and Leo were supplementing their jobs—he as a schoolteacher and she as a Web designer—with their Madoff income. And around the circle we went, talking softly, as if we were at a funeral. Taj was in the most dire situation because she was living in a rented house she could no longer afford and her income came solely from her Madoff accounts. As a well-known Sufi teacher, she had been giving retreats and working for Sufi organizations without pay for many years. That night, we knew that our lives had changed irrevocably—none of us, even then, believed that we would ever get any money back—but we didn't know how. We were like the emperor penguins in Antarctica, huddled together for body warmth and temporary comfort.

For those first few days after Madoff's confession, living in my mind was like trying to run on broken glass. I'd wake up in the middle of the night in terror. I'd walk into the guest room, where Kim was sleeping—she was always awake—and we would curl up together, crying, talking. When I wasn't crying, I desperately wanted to turn back the clock ten years, two months, even two weeks. I wanted to know then what I knew now and make different decisions about what to do with our money. I wanted to have paid for our house in full and to have fixed the plumbing so that we could take indoor showers instead of showering outside in the cold. I wanted to have given more of our money to the National Resources Defense Council so that they could save the whales, to have bought a condominium for my mother and stepfather. I wanted to have put most of our money in T-bills and CDs. But since there was no way of going back in time, these thoughts left me crazed and hysterical. I understood for the first time why people cut themselves, banged into walls: It gave them a way to externalize the torture they were living through inside their own minds.

When I had exhausted the dreams of going back in time, I'd ricochet to the future: Could we sell our house in this market? Would we have enough money to buy a trailer, live in a trailer park? My friend Stephanie said we could move in with her, live in her six-by-eight-foot dining room. Was that actually big enough for a bed and two people? What would happen to our sixty-pound dog? And Matt. What if he got sick? What if I got sick? Where would we go? What would we do? What if Matt died on the way home from Antarctica and I was alone in this mess?

Because the situation was so dire and the suffering of a raging mind so apparent, it became obvious that when I allowed my mind unfettered access to my thoughts, living inside my skin was unbearable. My thoughts evoked feelings that created bodily sensations. Panic. Terror. Self-blame. Rage.

Since I knew Matt was coming home in two weeks, I didn't put figures on paper. I didn't grocery shop. I didn't eat out. I didn't do anything but stay home, take walks with Kim, learn the "Kindness" poem by heart, open cans of sardines, and eat eggs on toast.

Within four or five days, I realized that my suffering was exactly equal to the things I told myself. No matter what Bernard Madoff had stolen, no matter what I had lost or what I had left, I could only suffer to the degree that I allowed myself to fly off the ragged cliffs of my mind.

I became vigilant about pulling my mind back from the brink of panic every time it wandered, which was thousands of times a day. Every time I noticed that I was starting to wind up the story of "what will I do, where will I go, what will happen to me, us," I stopped. Just stopped. Every time I started imagining making different decisions than I'd made two or ten years ago, I'd yank myself back to the present. And when my mind ran off without me, when I wasn't fast enough to catch the jump into the past or future, the subsequent anxiety or panic reminded me to bring myself back.

Life became incredibly simple; I saw that I had two choices: suffer unbearably or stay in the present moment. Anxiety was a reaction to my thoughts of the past or future. Panic was a reaction to my thoughts of the past or future. Hysteria was a reaction to my thoughts of the past or future.

In this moment—despite having lost thirty years of savings—I could still breathe.

In this moment I could still see.

In this moment there were still trees and wind and ground

and birds. I had legs and arms and chocolate. (Maybe not the 82 percent Venezuelan kind with notes of vanilla and cherry, but I could still afford a Hershey's kiss.)

In this moment, when I began paying attention to what I did have instead of what I didn't, there was a constant, unavoidable display of gorgeousness everywhere, anywhere.

In this moment, sufficiency could not be denied.

It's not that there weren't decisions to be made and lessons to be learned. It's not that something huge hadn't happened. It's just that in this *exact* moment, in the kitchen or backyard or car, there was no catastrophe. I had a roof over my head, food to eat, air to breathe. My house wasn't being bombed, and no one in the room was being raped or murdered. As long as I could breathe and sense and feel and see, I could bring my attention back to the fact of legs wind teacup hummingbird fingers computer. And each of those things was already whole and intact.

As the writer and Buddhist teacher John Tarrant has written about financial loss: "The sun still shines and you still drink your coffee and the birds still call in the morning. . . . You can find out that what you came to this planet for is not necessarily your apartment."

When my friend Sally used to tell me, "Suffering is a choice," I'd say, "It's easy for you to say. You had a mother who you knew adored you and so you came into this world believing that everything would work out. That even the bad times would turn into good times. But it's not like that for most of us. We don't believe that things will turn out well, because they haven't. Our suffering is real!"

"Choosing not to suffer" did not seem like an option; it felt superficial and naive, like those who say that if you wish for a new Jaguar, it will be yours—paste an affirmation on your mirror and soon you will believe it. Not me. I believed in darkness, shadows, subterfuge. Although I'd spent many years practicing meditation and inquiry, it became apparent that my fundamental loyalty was to suffering. But the enormity of the Madoff loss seemed to catapult me into understanding that I really did have a choice about how to live with what had happened.

Within a few weeks after the news broke, and after countless hours of bringing my attention back to the present when it wandered into the past or future, I felt settled in myself. Verging on happy.

During the third post-Madoff week, my mother called and asked me how I was doing.

"Great," I said. "I'm feeling pretty happy."

"Really?" she said. "Happy?" she asked. Then, in a voice tightened with worry, she said, "Sweetheart, I'm going to ask you a question and please tell me the truth. I won't blame you no matter what you answer."

"Okay, Mom. What is it?"

"Are you on drugs?"

"No, Mom," I laughed. "Not on drugs."

"Well, then tell me your secret. Tell me how it's possible

that you lost all your money just a few short days ago and you are happy now. And after you're done telling me, could you bottle it? Because I am sure you could make back all the money you lost if you did."

• • • • •

That's the thing about attention and awareness, about spiritual practice, that's so hard to explain. It's like, as Pema Chodron writes, "sitting at the Grand Canyon with a grocery bag over your head" and suddenly realizing that you have the choice to take it off. The world becomes instantly brighter, wider, breathtaking. As if you've been transported to what feels like a rainbow universe that includes the paper bag but also includes big sky and coiling rivers and clouds that look like God's cheeks. It is such a radical change from believing that life is what you can see from the inside of a paper bag that it seems unbelievable, impossible. And if you try to describe it to a brown-bag person, they might think you are crazy. Or that you are denying the existence of pain. They'll tell you that the switch to seeing rivers and cumulus clouds and jade green canyon walls is too quick, too soon, that it can't be real.

Since, in my own case, I'd been relentless about exploring my mind, particularly the scary places—the fears and the obsessions I'd been plagued by for years—the pathways to awareness and gratitude were somewhat established. And so was the steadfastness that was needed to return to them a thousand times a day. It wasn't an impossible leap to keep dragging my attention back from terror to presence, from blame to curiosity, from panic to gratitude. Which isn't to say that it wasn't difficult; it was. I often felt as if I were trying to yank a magnet away from steel filings. As if the seduction of blame and anxiety were a siren call that I could barely resist. But after so many years of practice, the commitment to the process was already there.

I also had constant support—I talked to Jeanne, Catherine, and Taj every day. When my mind jumped off the cliffs of panic, I picked up the phone and called one of them. I had a context, a community in which awareness about beauty, loss, and what I still had was more valued than ramping myself up into terror or spiraling down into depression and victimhood.

Although I had a well-established practice, there were many pre-Madoff moments when I still wondered if spirituality was a fancy description for self-indulgent navel gazing. But after we lost our money, I saw that what I was calling "spirituality"—the dedication to bringing my mind back to the present moment and slicing through the trance of my usual stories to the ground of goodness beneath them—was not a luxury, but a necessity.

Within a few post-Madoff weeks, I trusted that my primary commitment was not to Matt or my family or my work but to using whatever happened (good or bad) to bring myself back to the stillness beneath and between the passing thoughts. And that when I did, it always—100 percent of the time—resulted in gratitude and kindness (to myself and others).

After we lost our money, I understood in a visceral way

that there wasn't one thing that existed outside the story my mind constructed of it; I was always interpreting what I saw, felt, experienced through the filter of my own mind, fitting this moment into to an already existing frame of reference. An already existing story. A disaster that had happened forty years ago. I understood that as long as I could question what I was telling myself, I didn't need to be frightened of losing anything, even my life.

I still wasn't sure how we would live or where. And it was clear that the teeny issue of my relationship with money, my tendency to stockpile sweaters and earrings, and my belief that I could prosper while others were flailing had to be examined. But without my loyalty to suffering, examining my beliefs and behavior felt like riding a Ferris wheel on a lush summer day.

2

On a Shopping Binge

We're in New York for a few days and I want to shop. Never mind that we lost thirty years of life savings to Bernie Madoff or that we still owe the bank seventy thousand dollars on our home equity loan and hundreds of thousands of dollars on our mortgage. When facts as flimsy as bank loans meet the need to shop, they dissolve like water on a sizzling frying pan.

I try to reason with myself. "Self," I say, "it's not a good idea to go shopping right now. You will only see something—probably many things—you love: a pair of glittery ballerina flats, a fabulous jacket, the perfect purse with nifty pockets for phone, pens, even a slot for lipstick—and you will convince yourself that you have to have them. Glittery ballerina flats are not a priority right now; saving your house is. Get a grip."

It doesn't work. In this moment, I don't care about losing

my house. I don't care about going broke or home equity loans. I especially don't care about what can never be lost or how much I still have or the feeling of riding a Ferris wheel on a summer day. The luscious world of things awaits me; it is full of beauty and dark enchantment, ripe with invitations to turn my ordinary life into the life of my dreams.

Matt suggests going to a museum, a matinee, a movie. Is he kidding? I tell him I just want to "stroll down Madison Avenue. Look in the windows. See what Simon Doonan, the window designer for Barney's, has created this month." I tell him it inspires me that Simon is able to do so much with objects like smashed-up soup cans and birdcages and old phonographs. That it opens the world of invention, creativity, art, and since I am writing a new book, it will be helpful to be inspired. He gives me a "yeah, right" look but drops the subject anyway. It's sort of like those moments when he used to ask if what I was wearing was new, and although it usually was a purchase I'd recently made, I'd look down at my body with incredulity. "This old thing? I've had it for months!" He gives me *the look* and turns back to checking his e-mails. He seems to know that getting in the path of a rocket after it's launched does not yield positive results.

I kiss him good-bye, grab my purse, leave the room. Down the elevator, through the noisy lobby filled with businessmen in navy blue suits and tourists with Lululemon shopping bags and out onto the street. I run across Sixth Avenue just as the light is turning red and the taxis are gearing up to charge down the street. Anything (even, it seems, taking the chance of getting run over) to get to the stores three minutes faster.

I have no particular destination in mind, not really. I like the T-shirts at the Gap, the shoes at Stuart Weitzman, the skirts at H&M, the eyeglasses at 20/20. I walk fast, browsing in store windows as I move. I pass couples with their lips locked, women in black business suits and running shoes, homeless people and their dogs with signs that ask for help. On every block there are half a dozen people gesturing, talking loudly to the air, Bluetooth headsets plastered to their ears. I am anxious, hurried, guilt ridden. I don't want to shop and I have to shop. I don't want to find anything I want and my life depends on finding the It thing. *I know I shouldn't, I told myself I wouldn't, but I want to, I have to, I am going to.*

I am, it seems, on a binge.

As I run across yet another street when the light is turning red, I decide that I don't need another hat, purse, or T-shirt, but I do *need* another pair of glasses, since I've recently started wearing progressive lenses and I don't like my current frames. Feeling incredibly virtuous about everything I am not going to buy, I turn into a frame store and begin the hunting-and-gathering part of the expedition. The salesman hands me a pair of thick, black Clark Kent–looking glasses. He calls them the newest thing: geeky chic. "No way," I say as I point to a pair of light green frames with a stripe of red on the arms. Twelve pairs of frames later, I've found the ones that will change my life. The salesman—his name is Armand—calls them "crystal" because they have no color.

He says they pick up the light around my face and are just the right size, not too big, not too small. I strut shamelessly around the store, gazing like Narcissus at my reflection in the wall-to-wall mirrors. I imagine sweeping into assorted rooms, bedazzling everyone with my excellent taste in glasses.

Throngs of nameless other people are swarming around, crowding my fantasy. Each one of them seems to have nothing better to do with their time than to comment on my new eyeglasses. They all come to the same conclusion: Anyone who would wear glasses like mine is someone worth knowing, admiring, loving. As the fantasy progresses (it only takes about two minutes), Armand, like any savvy salesperson, functions as its narrator, murmuring that "it takes a certain kind of person to wear these frames. Someone original, someone creative. You must be an artist."

"How much?" I ask.

"Three hundred and forty-five dollars," he says. Without the lenses. And with the lenses? He takes out his calculator. With all the bells and whistles—thin glass, tinting, et cetera—it comes to close to a thousand dollars. I try not to gasp or appear shocked. I didn't know what I was planning to spend—the need to shop doesn't have to do with money; it has to do with fervor and fantasy and passion—but I know it wasn't a thousand dollars. Still, love magnets are not cheap. I tell him I have to think about it and will come back tomorrow.

Back on the street, I am aware that I've narrowly escaped the jaws of death by credit card, but my mind is still fixated on the frames. I zero in on particulars: see myself wearing them as I give lectures, teach workshops, appear on television. There is no situation that having those crystal glasses would not affect. As I walk to the restaurant where I am meeting my mother for lunch, I cut a path through people in black uniforms standing outside office buildings smoking cigarettes, poisoning the air with secondhand smoke. (*Gawd,* I think*, why can't they stop smoking? Why can't people have more control over their addictions?*) On every street corner there are stands selling five-dollar pashmina shawls, two-hundred-dollar knockoffs—I've checked—of Fendi Spy bags. Smells of diesel fumes, fried meat, hot pretzels conjoin to make the perfume I call Essence of New York.

My mother and I order lox, eggs, and onions with bagel chips and talk about my nephews, her bridge game, my upcoming lecture at the Beacon Theatre. All the while I am thinking about the crystal frames. I wish I already had them. I picture the outfit I am going to wear on Sunday to the Beacon, picture myself sauntering around the stage in my new glasses. No matter what we discuss—her friend who is dying, her sister who is having a knee replacement—I am either thinking about where I will wear the glasses or rationalizing spending a thousand dollars on something that is not rent or food.

My mother and I are shopping cohorts; she has her PhD in wardrobe selection, a skill she learned from her father, who had his silk underwear embroidered with his initials at Sulka, despite the fact that they were barely scraping by. I tell her about the glasses. "What about the pair you already have?" she asks. I am irritated at her question. What does stuff I already have have to do with these glasses?

It occurs to me to say, "Those old things?" but then I remember that because she was with me when I bought the glasses she's now asking about, she knows I've only had them for a year.

"You're missing the point, Mom," I say impatiently. (I don't know what the point is, but I know she's missing it.)

"Those are such great frames," she says. "How often have you worn them?"

"Twice," I say quietly. "They feel too big, too colorful. Like I am making a production every time I wear them. These—pointing to the ones I have on—are the only ones I wear." It doesn't occur to me to ask myself what is wrong with having only one pair of glasses. That question is so far from the frenzy of more-more-more that it is not even in the ballpark of consideration.

"You need to rethink this," my mother says. "I don't think this is about the glasses."

"Hello?" I say. "Are you the person who tells me she *needs* a new 'honey-colored purse' every six months?"

"I know, I know," she says. "But you're better than me. You can figure this out."

"Yeah, maybe," I say, "but in the meantime, will you come with me to look at these glasses?"

After our meal, we trudge down a few long blocks. Her back hurts—she's had two major operations in two years—and walking even a few steps is not easy. Still, my insistence, uh, obsession, lands us in the store. Armand welcomes us back as if he's known us forever, as if we were cousins arriving for a family reunion. I try on my new treasure. My mother says, "They look like goggles. They're terrible. The ones you have are so much better." I usually trust my mother's aesthetic sense—at eighty years old, she is still a knockout—but goggles? I remind her of the gold lamé gloves she once bought me, the ones that found a home at Goodwill.

"Are you sure, Mom?" I say. "Maybe it's because they're so unusual."

"Unusual is one thing," she says. "Ugly is another."

I look at Armand. We pass a "What do mothers know?" look. I shrug. I say, "I'll still be back tomorrow."

That night is fitful, distracted. I see an old friend, eat dinner at Chipotle, and all the while the crystal frames are haunting me. I know enough about compulsion to ask myself what I would be thinking about if I wasn't thinking about the glasses, but I can't come up with any satisfying answers. The usual questions I ask my students when they tell me they've been bingeing—*Did something happen? Were you feeling hurt or lonely or frightened?*—don't apply. I didn't feel restless or hurt about anything before I decided to shop, but I do notice that thinking about the glasses excites me, focuses me. It's as if life was bumping along at a humdrum pace and is now elevated to a heightened, electric state by the introduction of a new, gorgeous thing. Is it the thing I want or is it the aliveness? I don't seem to care enough to discern the difference. The pull toward buying something new is absorbing and compelling; it is like a gnawing in my chest that won't quit until the glasses are mine.

The next day, Matt and I are returning from breakfast and I decide to tell him about the glasses and the sheer amount of energy I am spending thinking about them. Will he come with me to look at them? Since we will be passing the store in about thirty seconds, he says, "Two minutes, that's it. Two minutes and I'm out of there." I know that bringing my mother and Matt to see the glasses is part of the dance of obsession; it's as if their presence validates (okay, enables) the out-of-control, divorced-from-reality fantasy in which I am engaged. But I can't stop now; I am like a freight train zooming downhill without brakes.

My new best friend, Armand, is standing behind the counter when Matt and I walk in. My eyes are glinting (if eyes could salivate, that's what mine would be doing) as he brings out the glasses. Before I can even get them on my face, Matt says, "Sweetheart, even if they were the last pair of glasses in the world and you had to crawl on all fours because you couldn't see, I'd tell you not to buy them. They look like goggles, like you should be snorkeling with schools of fish, not walking around in crowds of people."

Matt has a tendency to talk and live in huge brushstrokes—for example, he cracked an egg over his head once when we were in the middle of a fight as a way to end the argument—and my first impulse is to dismiss his comments. Snorkeling? Gimme a break. But since he and my mother said the same thing, it makes it the teeniest bit harder to dismiss his comments. Armand does the windup for the creative-daring-courageous thing, but it's too late: Two minutes is up. Matt and I walk through the revolving door and into the secondhand-smoke, Fendi-knockoff streets of Manhattan.

As we walk back to our hotel, Matt begins to chatter about his upcoming meetings that day. I listen with half a heart. The other half is thumping and flailing about the eyeglasses; I feel let down, deflated. Not only because he has the nerve to talk about something besides *me* but because without the purchase of the glasses to look forward to, I feel like I am being exiled in the parched desert of ordinary life. The speech I am giving in less than twenty-four hours doesn't seem to count as an attention grabber.

On our last day in New York, I return to the store, in part because I told Armand I'd be back, and also because I am still magnetized by the fantasy of my bedazzling glasses. When I walk into the store, a Frenchwoman named Juliet, the same person who waited on me when I bought the frames I do not wear, is standing at the counter. The first thing she says when she sees me is that a friend sent her my *Salon* piece on Madoff. "I loved it," she says. "It really touched me." At first I feel bright, happy: She liked the article. She found it helpful. How wonderful. Then I remember I am having this conversation because I seem to have forgotten what I'd learned by writing the article.

I am suddenly embarrassed by the entire situation: that I

am shopping again after losing so much money, that I bought two pairs of glasses a year ago and am back for more, that my hunger for things is bottomless. But before I have a chance to wallow in my shame, Juliet says, "Armand told me you put a pair of frames aside. Let's take a look."

Oh good, I think, *I'm released from having to have integrity.*

"Wow," she says, "these are nothing like the ones you bought before. These sort of look like goggles." She really said that, I swear.

Juliet continues. "The ones you already have are so beautiful—why would you want these?"

I flip through the many answers to that question:

Because I don't pay attention to what I do have, only to what I don't have?

Because I have no reference point for "enough"?

Because buying things gives me something to look forward to, something that makes me forget my incredibly privileged life?

Because having a "relationship" with Armand is like having an ersatz one-person crowd who, although getting paid to fawn over me, is supplying me with *wow*s for the day?

Because shopping allows me to be completely self-absorbed and thinking about other people or wars or poverty is so messy and inconvenient?

Because I'd rather exist in a fantasy world where goggles are love magnets than see that I already have what I need?

Another customer walks in the door wearing a cluster of

gold necklaces that clink like wind chimes. I tell Juliet to go ahead and help her. I'll wait.

Just this morning a friend sent me an interview in which a financial expert asked one of his clients whether she could actually afford the fancy barbecue she wanted to buy. And despite my descent into eyeglass insanity, I know that the real question (for me) is not only affordability. Once you have enough money to pay for housing, food, medical bills, basic clothing, it's about something much more elusive than whether you can afford a fancy barbecue, a bracelet, a vacation to Tahiti: What you value. What you really want.

It was so much easier to unwind the obsession with food. When I was fat, I thought the point of being thin was finally being able to eat coffee ice cream and white, powdery doughnuts all day long and not gain weight. But when I started losing weight by not dieting, I began to understand that even though I could eat rice pudding for breakfast, I wouldn't be able to think straight afterward if I did. It wasn't about what I could (afford to) eat; it was about connecting eating with something bigger than my desires of the moment.

During my years of dieting and bingeing, I saw my body as a thing I could throw around, an empty trash can into which I could stuff whatever my mind wanted to eat. As if what I ate and the body that received it were not related. But then I started to understand that eating was not about being fat or thin; it was a physical means, a path, to being more—or less—alive. I could use food to feel energetic, or I could use it to feel dead. I could jack myself up on a sugar high for half an hour and drag myself around for the rest of the day, or I could eat something that would actually give me energy instead of taking it away. It depended on whether and how much I valued feeling as alive as possible.

If that's what money is as well—if it's a means to connect what I value with what I spend—it seems that I am still at the white-powdery–doughnuts stage of financial wisdom. I don't yet believe—or at least I don't act as if I believe, so what's the difference?—that living is not about accumulating or that love is not something I can accomplish or control. I still act as if I believe that things have inherent meaning rather than the meaning I (and the culture) give to them.

Juliet is back, and for some reason that I can't quite track, the bubble of the obsession has been pierced and I begin to notice something other than myself: Juliet. I notice the feathery lines around her eyes, the fine lines above her mouth; her meadowy face looks like it's been through childbirth and illness. I notice that her skin has a faint smell of lilacs and reminds me of May in the Berkshires and the Sting song "Fields of Gold." I notice the turquoise paisley scarf she has tied around her waist in that offhanded and impossibly stylish way that only Frenchwomen seem to be able to pull off. I notice that she has dropped saleswoman speak and is trying to reach me, connect with me in a real way.

I look down at the crystal frames. I wanted them to be my ruby slippers, but everyone else (except Armand) saw that they were just goggles. I am reminded of a John Tarrant quote I memorized years ago and have written about before: "All wanting—for love, to be seen for who we are, for a new red car—is wanting to find and be taken into the mysterious depth in things."

Our plane is leaving in three hours and I have to get back to the hotel. I thank Juliet, kiss her three times—the way my European friends have taught me—and step out into the wilderness of New York. A purple-haired kid holding a basket is sitting on the corner with a sign that says: "Will work for iPhone." Since I've just saved a thousand dollars, I put five dollars in his basket and continue to my hotel.

3

Hyperventilating at Target

After my trip to New York, I stopped doing anything related to shopping (window-shopping, walking into stores, roaming the Internet for sales) for almost a year. I didn't want to go through the should-I-shouldn't-I hoopla, and I didn't want to drag all sentient beings within my immediate reach to the store. Although I realized that imposing a moratorium on shopping was a bit like fasting—eventually you have to eat/shop again and deal with the stuff around either or both—I decided to give myself a rest. Also, there was the matter of our mortgage to pay. And the teeniest issue of already having enough; it's difficult to ignore and humbling to admit (although I do a valiant job) that, except for food and gas and replacing underwear with holes, I wouldn't *need* to shop for adornments again. Ever.

Then, two nights ago, my friend Jane and I were going to a

lecture in San Francisco and wandered into a store nearby. "I can't believe how gorgeous every single thing is in this place," Jane said, breathless. She pulled out a gold angora sweater, then a long heather gray mohair tunic with rosettes appliquéd on each side. I touched an ankle-length brown wool dress with a flouncy hemline that I couldn't believe I had lived without this long. Then I flipped through a rack of jackets, each of which was more heart-stoppingly gorgeous than the last. An array of asymmetrical designs, puffy, shiny pieces, unusual fabrics—all of which looked like liquid love formed into long sleeves and a square shell. Then I looked at the price tags. I didn't have my one pair of glasses on and the numbers were hazy, out of focus.

"What does this say?" I asked Jane. She didn't have her glasses on either, and we stood there for a moment holding the tag three feet away from our faces.

"I think it says eight hundred dollars," Jane said.

"What about this one?" I asked, bringing over the dress I could no longer breathe without.

"Four hundred dollars," she said.

"Let's get out of here," I sputtered. My stomach was tight, my mouth salivating. I felt like one of my retreat students, who wrote to me that she hyperventilates when she shops anywhere, even at Target.

Jane nodded her head dreamily while fingering a purple shearling vest. "Isn't this the living end?" she asked. "Isn't this amazing?"

"It is," I answered, tugging on her shirt. "Now let's go." I was starting to feel as if I were alternately swooning and suffocating with desire.

As we walked to the restaurant, I said, "I'm so glad we got out of there. I felt like the body snatchers invaded my body. I could hardly breathe."

She laughed. "I think it was different for me than for you. I was overcome with the beauty, but I never felt as if I was in any kind of danger of buying anything. I live in a beach town. I wear flip-flops and baggy pants every day; I don't have a life in which I would wear anything in that store, but I still had to admire the workmanship and the fabrics. The outrageous splendor of it all. On the other hand, last week I couldn't stop myself from buying a huge—and very expensive—ceramic cross with tiny little roses all over it. After I saw it, I couldn't stop thinking about it. And then finally I gave in, went back, and bought it."

A rose-studded cross? Really? Although there are many reasons why rose-laden crosses hold no allure for me, it doesn't seem to matter what the object is; the process is the same for us Things People: You are bumping along in your life when suddenly you see something that you have to have. A moment before, you didn't know you needed it, but now that you've seen it, you can't take one more breath without it.

· · · · ·

When I read the shopping-for-goggles piece to my retreat students, I realized that I had been so immersed in the drama that

I had missed the punch line: how I used shopping to alter my state of mind during that aforementioned New York trip.

Tearing around Manhattan was, despite what ensued, an attempt to calm myself down. I'd given talks to large audiences before, but I'd never spoken at a grand New York theater like the Beacon, where Leonard Cohen had once appeared. Part nervous, part wild with excitement, I was rehearsing the sequence of the talk in the mornings when I awoke, when I jogged around Central Park, and again before I went to sleep. Shopping allowed me to completely distract myself from my overamped nervous system while at the same time re-creating familiar forms of contact. But since both the attempt to "regulate and self-soothe" (as psychologists say) and the re-creation of old ways of relating were based in the past and irrelevant in my current situation, they failed miserably.

The attempt to soothe myself by shopping left me feeling like a narcissistic wreck. In focusing on whether to buy the glasses or not, I reconstituted my old friend, obsession: I created a diversion from the present moment by focusing on something utterly irrelevant but completely absorbing and thereby created a secondary problem that occupied all my attention; I created a life on top of my life.

When we are obsessed with anything—food, drugs, alcohol, making or spending money—the obsession takes on a life of its own—and then defines how we spend our time, our energy, our resources. Obsession is a form of autism, a way to cover our ears and block out the background noise, a way to protect ourselves when the situation feels vulnerable or dangerous or anxiety producing. Obsession is a way to change the channel when you don't like what's barreling across the screen of your mind.

Focusing on food and weight and calories was lifesaving for me when family dynamics were intolerable. But focusing on a thousand-dollar pair of glasses when we had recently lost our savings was a bit out of touch. If an adult rather than an eight-year-old had been occupying my body, another alternative would have been to rehearse my talk and relax rather than rehearse and then whip myself up into wild-eyed hysteria. But that would have required a level of awareness that I lacked—and had no desire to cultivate—at that moment.

Then there was the wee issue of reeling in my mother and my husband so they could participate with me in the drama. Talk about re-creating the past. When I think of happy times as a kid, I don't think of holidays or family dinners or recitals or being read to at night; I think of stores. My Darling Daughter. Young Years. Helen May. Bloomingdale's, Gee Gaw, Clothes N' Things. It was there that I felt as if I mattered, there, in those stores, that I counted. That I had my mother's attention and my father's.

I practically lived for the ritual of setting the time to shop, looking forward to the appointed day, getting in the car, driving together, going through the racks of clothes. Trying them on. Parading around the store in a new outfit. Taking it off, trying on another, then another. Talking about what to buy, what not to buy. I wanted to stretch the time, keep trying on clothes, keep talking so that we wouldn't have to go home. I wasn't as interested in what we bought as in the oasis of time that shopping allowed us.

Buying was a letdown. Buying meant the end, being let go, cut off, released into the madness again—and into the wilds of my own loneliness. Which explains the relentless foreplay to the goggle buying. It wasn't the glasses I wanted, although I didn't know that at the time; I wanted the activity—the "bonding" around picking out, talking, deciding, talking again, redeciding. To the part of me bent on survival, relating to my mother and husband about the purchase was the very definition of togetherness, of comfort, of love—and when it stopped, any semblance of connectedness would stop as well.

It's both painful and humbling to see the extent to which I am still and unconsciously driven by the imperatives of a chubby, utterly lost eight-year-old. It's as if these habits, beliefs, and what a mentor of mine calls "couplings" have a life of their own.

When I couple human relatedness—and to a child relatedness means the difference between living and dying—with the activities of shopping, I will be gripped, taken over, helpless to do anything but react and consume. At those moments, my life belongs to the unconscious associations I've made, the particular way my psyche has equated love with buying, stillness with despair. Survival trumps good intentions every time. When the imperative to shop (or eat or drink or take drugs) takes over, nothing else exists. It's why diets don't work, budgets get thrown out, credit-card debt keeps accumulating. The momentary imperative of survival will always, in every situation, hijack long-range perspective.

And alas, the only way through this morass of imperatives is awareness itself. Which means that instead of reacting in the same ways to the same needs, I begin widening the perspective. I realize I have other choices. I use my mind and the ability to be aware of thoughts, beliefs, and feelings to name the patterns each time they arise. Once I am aware of what is driving my behavior that was previously unconscious (and removed from my awareness), I can begin to decouple associations that, while laminated together, have nothing to do with each other.

According to neuroscience, when we associate love with shopping for twenty or thirty years, or when we pair any kind of discomfort—anxiety, boredom, fear, loneliness, sadness—with danger (fragmenting, collapsing, falling apart), neural pathways get established in the brain; our responses to situations will endlessly follow those same pathways until we establish new ones. Until we uncouple shopping from connectedness or anxiety from danger, we will repeat the same behaviors again and again. I go to New York (the very place where these couplings were first created) to work, and without thinking, I suddenly need to shop.

The problem with decoupling is that it takes awareness. It takes time. It takes willingness to tolerate discomfort. It takes motivation to see through the patterns. It takes the courage to actually see that we don't want to see. It also takes confidence that it is possible to get to the other side. That there is something better than an immediate fix: knowing your own mind, contacting your own heart. Telling the truth. Understanding that feelings won't kill you.

When I asked my friend Grace, another Madoff investor, about shopping, she said, "When I feel out of control or bad, the simplest way to feel some control is to buy something pretty. I get to experience wanting it and then getting it. The world becomes simple, reduced, manageable. I like that."

"What do you think would happen if you just let yourself feel the 'badness' without having to distract yourself from it?"

"I don't want to find out," she said.

And that's what it comes down to: We don't want to find out. We don't want to feel the feelings at the source of the impulse to spend (or eat) because we believe those feelings would tear us apart. So although our financial situations may be dire, the truth is that we don't want to think about them. We decide, albeit unconsciously, that the pain of unconsciousness is better than the effort to increase awareness. Most of us have gotten so inured to the former that we no longer realize its cost. We've lived in the shade of unconsciousness for so long that we think that this is the way life is—and will always be. We've stopped believing in brightness.

When I asked one of my retreat students, a well-known alternative physician, about her financial situation, she said,

The first thing that comes up for me is enormous SHAME and TERROR: Shame that I make a lot of money (in my terms) and yet I hardly have any cash available to feel relaxed and confident to make purchases that are modest by most standards; and Terror that all I have will fall apart like a house of cards: three houses, two cars, a child in college, and credit-card debt. I feel the shame arise as I "confess" this. It's like telling someone what I've eaten today.

My debt has been a shameful secret, and like the visibility of weight, if it all crashes and I lose everything, I will be exposed as a fraud. This is what my cataclysmic anxiety tells me. I am unable to pay the IRS my estimated income tax payments and make my annual IRA contribution for the first time in thirty years of working. I cannot really work any more than I already do with so many patients in three offices.

And yet I experience budgeting as a form of dieting. Off and on, I pay attention to my spending the way I used to count calories, resolving each week to curb myself, and by the end of the week feel extremely exhausted and despairing that I haven't made a dent in the situation. I see that the shame is linked to despair. Despite my real estate portfolio, I experience myself as having no money because these are not liquid assets. (Now I am feeling guilty for even saying this because, in reality, and compared to most of the world, I have so much.)

> But I also realize that I have a hard time keeping money. If I have it, I find a way to spend it or give it away, usually in loans that never get repaid. In my practice, I let my clients run a tab, unable to feel entitled or unwilling to stop the treatment until they can pay. I suppose, all in all, I am saying that I'd just rather not think about any of this. Because thinking about it, and even saying this to you, brings up so many feelings of shame and fear.

It's as if we have lodged ourselves between two impossible choices: If I think about money, I will feel unbearably ashamed, restricted, exhausted, doomed, incapable. If I don't think about it, there's a chance I might lose it all. So we avoid the whole situation by doing what we've always done: blocking it out. Until a crisis is reached: We lose our jobs, we lose our houses, we lose our money.

Before the Madoff debacle, I kept resolving to examine my relationship with money. I'd think, *I really should pay attention to this. Something crazed comes over me when I walk into a store, something a bit scary. And why aren't I balancing my checkbook? Why do I immediately go into a foggy state whenever I am in the accountant's office?*

I'd be haunted by the fact that the way I spent money was not aligned with my beliefs about sufficiency, value, sustainability. Also, since my main philosophy about food was that we eat the way we live and that our relationship with food is a perfect mirror for our beliefs about abundance, scarcity, deprivation, joy, and nourishment, it made sense to me that my relationship to money was also a reflection of many parts of me—which, given my behavior, was not a comforting thought.

I spent years meditating, steeping in the understanding that I am not my body, not my personality, not my achievements, not my possessions, and still flipped into supermarket-sweep mode when I entered a store. Worse, as soon as I saw this disconnect between what I said I believed and what I spent, I'd feel deeply ashamed, ranting at myself about being politically and spiritually incorrect. But the shame and rants were themselves so painful that I'd rationalize my unconsciousness by saying, *I'm not going to understand everything in this life. I've dealt with my relationship with food. That's enough. Only God is perfect.*

Every once in a while, I'd wind myself up about the need to deal with my money mania in the same way that I used to wind myself up to go on a diet: I'd make an ironclad resolution to begin with what seemed like a little task—balancing my checkbook. But as I'd begin going through the motions of reconciling what I thought I had with what the bank said I had, I'd get more and more anxious. I'd rifle through the clutter on my desk, find the last few statements, spend hours tallying the monthly fees—and still never end up with the same number as the bank. Within a few hours, I'd feel frenzied and incapable and hopeless. I'd want to watch soap operas for thirty-six hours, take a yearlong bath, get a colonic irrigation (okay, maybe that's an exaggeration) to wash away the doom. One seemingly little task was charged with so many pulls—*I can't, I have to, I should, I don't want to, I need to do this, I need to rest*—that I'd go back to the "Only God is perfect" line and focus on tasks I could accomplish.

• • • • •

When I first started working with my own compulsive eating, it was like peeling off the top layer of my body. Although I'd been bingeing and dieting for seventeen years, I had never talked to *anyone* about my relationship to food. Oh yeah, I was a member of the Whiners and Diners; I'd commiserate with friends about my weight, speculate about the newest diets, gossip about who had lost weight and how. But I never considered looking at the underbelly of food and me—the darkness, the craziness, the times I'd taken pizza out of the garbage can, dusted it off, and eaten it. How compelled I was by bingeing. How violently I loathed myself. How much I wanted the whole thing to just go away.

Chögyam Trungpa Rinpoche, a Tibetan Buddhist teacher, said: "Ordinarily we don't let ourselves experience ourselves fully. We have a fear of facing ourselves. Many people try to find a spiritual path where they do not have to face themselves but where they can still liberate themselves. In truth, that is impossible. We have to be honest with ourselves. We have to see our gut, our real shit, our most undesirable parts."

It's usually not until we've tried everything else—which usually consists of various forms of denial, years of making and breaking resolutions, and trying desperately to pretty ourselves up—that we circle back to "our most undesirable parts." After years of dieting and bingeing and running in place, I realized that I could not free myself from the obsession with food without welcoming the feelings that prompted it. Sometimes that looked like standing at my refrigerator, bingeing on a gallon of ice cream with my fingers, and crying between bites. Feeling lonely, desperate, needy. Sometimes it looked like telling my secrets and realizing they no longer had the power to destroy me.

In my first book, *Feeding the Hungry Heart*, I wrote about names I was called in school: Pregnant-Faced Cow, Thunder Thighs, Little Miss Piglet. I'd never told anyone about those names because I still believed they were true. And I remember thinking that when the book came out, people would begin calling me those names again. They'd realize I was a fake. They'd use my secrets against me. But I also knew that until I was willing to stop hiding what I believed were the scariest, ugliest parts of myself, freedom from the obsession was not possible.

As huge as the secrets, fogginess, craziness, shame, terror around food are, it seems that they are magnified in the relationship with money. My best friend from high school has told me her darkest secrets for forty years: We've lived through the deaths of her brother and her father, her sister's addiction to drugs, her compulsive eating. But it wasn't until last month, when we met over lunch in New York, that she told me that she's thirty thousand dollars in credit-card debt—and has been for the last ten years.

"Why didn't you tell me this before?" I asked.

"Because I was too ashamed. I didn't want to see myself as someone who was this out of control. It's not even that I spent the money on big things. I spent it on clothes, candles, gizmos, shoes. Impulse buys. And I kept telling myself that next month, I would begin paying it back. But then I never did. I kept carrying the debt over, and the interest kept growing."

When I first started working with eating disorders, no one was talking about their fears, their shame, the way they connected food with love. But the reluctance to talk about money is even more entrenched than the reluctance to talk about food. It seems that people will talk about anything—dry vaginas, penile dysfunction, five-thousand-calorie binges—before they'll talk about how they spend money.

After the death of my friend Reba's mother, her family sat shivah—the Jewish version of an Irish wake. When one of Reba's Catholic friends visited the shivah, she asked what the protocol was. "What am I supposed to talk about or not talk about?" the friend asked.

And Reba's uncle Manny said, "Anything goes here. Just don't talk about money. Not because it's part of the shivah rules but because it makes people uncomfortable."

· · · · ·

A retreat student writes:

> I struggle with feeling insufficient and incompetent. I wonder if I'm enough, if this life is enough. I long for a magical fix, whether it be a million dollars or the perfect body or a beautifully imperfect perfect relationship (or all three) that can deliver me the freedom and rest that I long for. But then I imagine having all those things, and I still feel heavy and indecisive. And then I realize that I keep fighting the heaviness, the messy feelings. I realize it's time to look at these feelings, be with them. Understand them. And then I go buy a new coat instead.

Changing longtime patterns and behaviors is a process, not a onetime event; even after I lost weight, it took years before I understood that acknowledging and working with what Trungpa calls my "real shit" was itself part of the freedom. When I wasn't hiding anything any longer, when I wasn't trying desperately to appear sane or put together or profound, I had nothing to lose. And I began to trust something even more fundamental than my craziness: my basic sanity.

But for now, it seems, I have to go through the process again: realizing something is slightly mad in my psyche where money is concerned. This requires a reasonable amount of ego humbling because it names the truth: I am a mess the second I walk into a store. But once I see that I am a mess, I feel instantly better because I no longer have a self-image to protect and I can start being interested in the truth.

The next step—understanding the couplings I've made between love and shopping, between being nervous and falling apart, between my self-worth and my net worth—requires a bit of fortitude because it too is uncomfortable. But as I tell my students, it's not exactly like we get to choose between ecstasy and discomfort and, in the name of awareness, become masochists and choose discomfort. *We're already in discomfort.* We're already in credit-card debt. We're already leveraged to the hilt. We're already using money/shopping as a drug—it's just that now we are naming it and are willing to tolerate the helplessness or heaviness or emptiness or neediness at its source.

Here's what I know from direct experience: In the middle of what seem like our darkest, craziest patterns is a ground of basic sanity and basic goodness that is untarnished and indestructible. The Buddhists call it Buddha-nature. The Christians call it Christ consciousness. The Taoists call it the Way of the Tao. But what it feels like to me is untarnished love, brightness, vastness, benevolence. That's where unpacking the craziness around food brought me. That's where it brings my students. Out of the garbage grows flowers, says Thich Nhat Hanh. When there is more garbage to be revealed, there are more flowers. It's true every time.

4

Dieting and Bingeing, Budgeting and Splurging

Until Madoff's confession, I didn't realize that I felt exactly the same way about money as I once had about food: I wasn't allowed to have either. Not really.

First, the food: Eating, I was convinced, was for skinny people. Eating was for men and boys. Eating was for those who didn't have to atone for their existence by sacrificing or depriving themselves. During the years I dieted and binged, I was convinced that real eating—food that tasted good—was breaking the law. When I stopped dieting, as I've written before, I felt as if I were committing heresy. The good kind. As if I were shouting to God, my mother, and my ex-boyfriend Tom (who said my thighs were too fat) that *I was allowed!* I was allowed to take up space! I was allowed to have pleasure, have needs, say what I wanted.

Since I was then twenty-eight and had been dieting for more than half my life—seventeen years—the only way I knew to accomplish this was to eat what I *hadn't* allowed myself to eat—fattening foods that only men and thin people ate. Chunky cookies and pumpkin ice cream and four-cheese pizza. After a few weeks of vacillating between nausea and giddiness, there was a clunk, a shift in my attitude: I understood that food wasn't good or bad and eating wasn't about right or wrong or being loved or rejected. It was only about this body—my body—and figuring out what it needed to move, think, thrive. Removing judgments from food made eating much simpler; it's not that my crazy eating suddenly disappeared, it's that when my perspective shifted, and my orientation was about what gave my body energy versus what drained it, decisions about cheesecake or ice cream slowly lost their fraught, hysterical quality. Eating became a way to sustain and support my body, not the way I was either trying to prove I was worthy (by denying myself) or rebelling against the internal voice that told me I wasn't (by bingeing).

After Madoff confessed, I realized that I had transferred the same "not-supposed-tos" to my relationship with money: I wasn't supposed to have it, I wasn't supposed to spend it, and if I happened to make it, I needed to pretend I hadn't. Every time, without exception, that I spent money on myself, I felt as if I were breaking the law. As if I were supposed to be on a diet and had just broken all the rules by stuffing down an entire cheesecake. I'd get anxious and begin going over and over the purchases the way I used to go over and over my intake of food: *Did I really need these flowers, that book, those boots? Aren't there better things to do with money than to spend it on myself? What about the whales? The polar bears? The women who are getting raped in Congo?* In the same way that I used to hide what I ate so that no one would see me with a bag of potato chips or a carton of ice cream, I was ashamed of making and spending money.

And just as I yearned to lose weight but believed that being thin—and the power associated with it—would threaten other people, I believed that it was fine to talk about money as long as I didn't let myself or anyone else know that I had very much. Otherwise, they (whoever they were) would be threatened by me—and leave. My unspoken conviction was that being thin and/or having money evoked hatred, envy, and backstabbing—and since I wanted to be loved and accepted, my choices seemed to be lose weight and lose friends or stay fat and be loved. Also: have money and be hated or be poor and be accepted.

But I soon discovered a third option: losing weight but hiding my body. Making money but pretending I didn't. As my body got smaller, my clothes got larger—baggy pants, shapeless tops, tentlike dresses. And when I began making more money than I could spend on food, rent, gas, and sweaters, I often devolved into a ditzy, confused child who needed an adult to take care of finances. I bought things I didn't need, gave extravagant gifts hoping secretly to buy love, and shoved the money part of our lives onto Matt. After we were introduced to B.M., I signed over every check I received to my

Madoff account and thereby removed myself from the onus of and responsibility for financial decisions.

My belief underneath all the other beliefs was that women—I—needed to hide, or at least tone down, the shine, the luminosity, the power; otherwise I'd be hunted, burned at the stake of other people's envy. This wasn't a conscious belief. I never thought, *I'm wearing a tent dress today because I don't want anyone to see my body and be threatened.* Or *I need to get rid of my money quickly because if anyone knew how much I had, they would hate me.* The fear of being fully myself—plus the many ways I learned to hide—manifested as a familiar way of being in the world: slightly off balance, easily overwhelmed, and perpetually exhausted. I was convinced, albeit unconsciously, that I could not be fully myself without apology.

Slowly, after I saw what I did with food and money (and in my relationships with friends, my husband, and other people, because when a pattern is active in my psyche, it gets acted out everywhere), I began to question not just the consequences of my actions—losing my money, wearing pants that could fit me and three other people—but also the combination of feelings and beliefs that were at the bottom of them, particularly the imperative to hide, sneak, or otherwise cut myself down in ever more creative ways.

My friend Linda told me about a money class she had taken with a group of women starting their own businesses. The instructor once asked them to imagine creating a thriving business. After spending some time on the number of employees they would need and their ideal amount of monthly traffic, she asked them to imagine how much money their companies could generate if they were "extravagantly successful." Then she told them that this money—their money—would be waiting for them in an imaginary bank during the break. They were then instructed to retrieve the cash and bring it back for the second half of the class.

Linda told me that of thirty women, only two women actually went to the "bank" and got their cash. The rest of the class forgot. They just forgot. Although they were taking the class because they said they wanted to be successful, they felt "funny" or "ashamed" or "concerned that other people wouldn't have made as much, and then what?"

Most of us have become so accustomed to acting out our internal version of ourselves that we are no longer aware that just because we believe something doesn't make it true. Just because we've been living according to particular beliefs for twenty or fifty years does not mean they have one shred of validity, as Richard, whose family had been investing in Madoff for decades, discovered on December 11, 2008. Our lives, our behaviors, our feelings—particularly about food and money—are like the Madoff charade; they're built on distortions, and after a while the whole system becomes so entangled that it takes a dedicated commitment to understand and replace it with current-day reality.

• • • • •

Since both food and money—nourishment and worth—are inextricably woven into the fabric of love and lack of love, they trigger feelings of deprivation, abundance, sufficiency, giving, receiving, entitlement, needs, wants, pleasure, suffering—and survival itself. And although there are many real problems about food and money, especially in third-world cultures and here during the recent recession, most problems about food or money are not about either one. Our relationships to both substances are expressions of unconscious beliefs, family messages, outdated convictions, and painful memories that most of us would rather walk on burning coals than examine.

I took my relationship with food to such an extreme—dieting, fasting, eating only raw food, becoming anorexic, then gaining eighty pounds in two months and being a few days away from killing myself—that taking another breath literally depended on understanding what I was doing. And so I made it my life's work to demystify the obsession. Or, as my brother says, "Most people just suffer, but you make a career out of it."

My relationship with money was easier to ignore because I avoided credit-card debt, adjusted my expenses to my various income-producing activities—whether it was sandwich making or workshop leading—and was able to get by with a little ignorance and a lot of privilege. Since I became inexplicably anxious whenever I spent money, and since no matter what I had I believed I never had enough, I knew that something was terribly off, but I also knew how to push the conflicts aside and distract myself with other parts of my life.

When Madoff confessed, I was faced with the financial equivalent of my early relationship with food: disaster. The shock of losing every penny of life savings, coupled with my ignorance, greed, and obvious unconsciousness, shattered my financial haze. Any shred of hubris about having thoroughly, completely, once and for all dealt with the issues at the root of my relationship with food was gone. Because here they were/are again, in a different form: the same shame about being myself, the same tendency to hide, to lie, to stockpile. The same feelings of not having enough while refusing to see how much I actually had on my plate or in my closet. The same pattern of rebelling (by bingeing and spending) against restriction and then getting so frightened of being out of control that I restricted myself again by dieting and budgeting.

In my previous books I've written that I believed that everyone in the West has a shtick with food; even the people who aren't compulsive have their own food-related quirks. But diving into the money arena has opened up a vast solar system of shtick. Just ask someone at a party how much money they made that week or month or year, just mention the word *money*, *budget*, or *finance* and you'll see fear, panic, shame, outrage, collapse, bluster, obstreperousness. Everyone, without exception, has money "issues"—and most of them range from slightly crazy to very crazy. It seems that money, even more than food, activates our survival instincts and makes wise, otherwise rational people behave like starving dogs. Any distorted or frozen patterns in our psyches will inevitably show up in our relationship with money, which makes it the ultimate repository for shadowy behavior. It also makes it the perfect place to explore the hidden conditioning that is running our lives.

Financial books are filled with tips about using cash not credit cards, diversifying your portfolio, understanding the difference between stocks and bonds, and investing in precious metals, just as diet books are filled with tips on when to eat and where, what to eat and why. Are our attitudes about food and money connected? One woman told me that if she could have the money back she's spent on diet books and weight-loss programs (that didn't change her behavior), she could make a down payment on her dream house. Sigh.

During the years I was investing in Madoff, I'd go through financial-literacy binges. I'd read a raft of authors, from Robert Kiyosaki to Suze Orman to Jacob Needleman. I'd consult financial advisers, read online columns, subscribe to economic newsletters. Not a dent. Oh yeah, I'd think about diversifying, talk about diversifying, worry about diversifying, but since the main pull was *not to think*, it was safer to feel poor, even with a million dollars in the bank. It was better to throw the money away than to make considered decisions about investing it. And even that's inaccurate because my "decisions" about which ways to think and behave were not conscious; I was running on conditioning so deeply rooted in my past that just hearing the word *money* sent me into a kerfuffle. Like hearing the word *food* once did.

• • • • •

At one of my retreats, a student said: "I am a saver. I get anxious when I spend money on myself. I grew up poor and have been saving pennies my whole life. It sends me into a frantic swirl to buy myself anything; I feel as if I need to save, save, save. I had wanted to see you at a retreat since 1999 and waited until 2007 to fly to California. Eight years went by and I didn't make myself or the expenditure a priority. I am the giver, the good girl with money. I have one pair of tennis shoes, and when they wear out, I will set a limit of how much I want to spend and shop until I find another pair for that price. My relationship with food is the same. I restrict and restrict, but then suddenly when I can't stand it anymore, I binge. At least when I binge I am not taking anything away from other people. At least I am giving something to myself. But the problem is that bingeing not only gives me something, it hurts me as well. I don't seem to be able to give myself anything without taking it away at the same time."

People binge on food or money because they believe they're not supposed to eat/have what they want. But just because you tell yourself you *shouldn't* eat six pieces of bread a day doesn't mean you stop *wanting* six pieces. And the more you tell yourself you can't have it—the more you want, think about, and obsess about it—the stronger the charge around the bread gets. Soon all you can think about is *needing* to eat that bread.

But something else happens as well: Since we are an interrelated system, it is virtually impossible to tell yourself something on the physical level that doesn't also affect you emotionally, psychologically, and spiritually. When you tell yourself that you can't eat what you want, you also tell yourself that you can't *have* what you want. That you can't be trusted. That you're out of control. That what you want will destroy you. And in my experience of working with compulsive eaters for thirty-three years, no one can tolerate hearing this for very long without reacting to it by either restricting themselves further or giving up the battle and bingeing. Or both.

The reason why compulsive eating and spending (including the compulsive need to restrict both) is so difficult to stop is that the cure does not address the problem. Almost every compulsive eater I know knows exactly what, when, and how much to eat.

Calories aren't the problem.

Exercise is not the problem.

Food is not the problem—it's only the middleman. It is the vehicle, the means, the transport for the internal sense of self—of value and worth, of deficiency and scarcity—to express itself.

The same is true with money.

Anaïs Nin said, "We don't see things as they are, we see them as we are." When you look at the world through the lens of not having enough, all you see is lack, hunger, emptiness. During the years we were invested with Madoff, I took countless walks with Matt during which I'd recite a litany of reasons why we didn't have enough money

"What if you suddenly have to stop working?" I'd say to Matt, wringing my hands. "What if I have to stop? What if there's an earthquake and our house gets destroyed and the insurance company won't pay?"

Matt would take a deep breath, tell me that we had more than enough for any emergency, that we were actually rich, but I didn't believe him. I couldn't hear him.

When you don't believe you're allowed to have what you have or want what you want, it doesn't matter how much money you have in your bank account. You are always poor.

When you are fat on the inside, you could be five feet ten and weigh 110 pounds and you'd still feel fat. And not just feel. You'd still believe you *were* fat.

You don't have to be anorexic to have a distorted body image. I've worked with radiant, accomplished women who spent hours trying to convince me that a particular bulge on their thighs or ripple of cellulite on their arms needed to be eliminated because it *meant something* about their existence, their inherent value on this earth.

It wasn't the cellulite; it wasn't the bulge; it isn't the money. It's the meaning we give to them—what we are convinced they express about our deepest vulnerabilities, fears, anxieties—that determines the quality of our lives.

Most of us walk around like the beggar in the Buddhist story who spent his life sitting on a mat with his hand outstretched, begging for a few alms a day without realizing that a trove of gold coins was buried in the dirt beneath his mat.

He never, not once, thought to look where he was already sitting.

When we see ourselves as beggars or starving-dog beings, we can't help but grope for more. This groping—in conjunction with our blindness to the reality of the present moment—is the definition of compulsion itself.

• • • • •

In my book *Women Food and God*, I describe two types of compulsive eaters: Restrictors and Permitters. Restrictors attempt to control their experience by depriving themselves. *If I cut myself off at the knees, I won't have far to fall when someone else brandishes the sword. If I take up as little space as possible, I won't be a target. If I don't get attached, I won't get hurt when people leave.*

Now, post-Madoff, I see that the same patterns of Restricting and Permitting apply with money. A Restrictor believes, *If I don't spend money, I won't have buyer's remorse. If I don't allow myself to be fully alive, dying will be less painful.*

Permitters numb themselves to their experience by getting lost in a fog of overeating and overspending. They use an idealized version of the future to fill the painful holes of their past. *What credit card? What mortgage? What hunger? What diabetes? Life is short. I can sleep and pay my bills when I'm dead, but right now, I want ice cream. And I need, I really need, an iPhone. I've worked hard. I deserve it. Carpe diem!*

Restrictors and tightwads control; Permitters and spendthrifts numb.

Each of us has a preferred mode of handling our feelings, and although it seems that Permitters have more fun, the truth is that both are defense mechanisms that have nothing to do with reality; both are reactions to events that happened decades ago, sometimes before we knew our own names. Which means that, for the most part, our relationships to food and money are reactive and unconscious. They are ways we express ancient, outdated beliefs about meaning and loving and living. About wanting and giving and receiving.

If a diet/budget could talk, it would say *I'm going to beat this [whatever "this" is]. I'm going to be good. I'm going to pull myself up by my bootstraps, discipline myself, and be the person I think I should be.*

If a binge/splurge could talk, it would say *Did you say that I'm not allowed to eat bread or buy that hat? Ha! I'm now going to eat the ENTIRE LOAF and move on to the crackers, chips, and tortillas. And if I am forced to limit what I eat, I am going to charge up a storm. NO ONE gets to tell me what I can and can't eat or buy. Got that? No one.*

As if someone were actually listening. As if we were either pleading with or shouting at an invisible and demanding authority figure. Or God.

One of my retreat students writes:

> I bounce from permitting to restricting with regularity. I work 12 hour shifts, sometimes many in a row, then have long stretches off. I eat this way too. Everything feels very extreme. My self-esteem waxes and wanes with the amount of money I am able to spend at

any given moment; my menu changes accordingly too. I start eating more junk because I "can't afford good food" and maybe because I feel like I don't deserve it. When I have a little money in my pocket though I eat REALLY good food, usually very fattening, going out to eat a lot. Because I deserve it! I start living beyond my means. No balance. I am always feeling empty and always trying to prove that I'm not.

As I've entered my own breathtakingly vast solar system of money shtick, I see that there are two interrelated parts in the demystification process: me and money/food. The me that I wake up as and in, and the money/food messages I learned from my family, my environment, and the culture.

Although my relationship to food developed in large part around mothering and the lack of it, and although food was an obsession for me long before I ever touched money, it wasn't the food itself or my perpetually fluctuating weight that was so painful; it wasn't even the relationship with my mother. As bits and pieces of early interactions, impressions, and family tones of voice coalesced, they formed an internal weather pattern, a way of looking at the world and my own place in it that I began to recognize as me. By the time I was ten or eleven, I had a recognizable "identity," a way of knowing myself that was familiar and automatic: I was selfish; I was needy; I was a pain in the ass. I was a kid whose own mother didn't want her.

From these core convictions a familiar sense of self developed that I began to believe was the absolute truth. It didn't matter that my mother did love me but felt unloved and lonely herself. I did the same thing every child does: blamed myself for the pain in my family and constructed an identity in the process—it's what psychologists call the process of ego formation. And because I carried this sense of self everywhere, it infused every relationship I had—with my brother, friends, boyfriends, teachers, food, and money.

As this familiar self, eating was against the law. Spending was against the law. Both were tinged with religiosity. When I was atoning for my existence, sweet things, good-tasting things, beautiful things were like the devil, tempting me to stray. I had to repent, not go around engaging in froufrous. Dieting on dry Grape-Nuts for six weeks was appropriate. Getting up in the mornings at five, meditating, walking, and being at my desk by eight, not taking a break until five in the afternoon. This was what I deserved. This was what people like me needed to do. I had to push beyond my capacity, work beyond exhaustion. I had to give, then give again. I had to make up for my basic deficiency by spending the time trying hard to improve myself, not eating ice cream or buying bracelets. For God's sake.

But.

Since I'm not a member of Opus Dei and since I sleep on a mattress, not a bed of nails, and since dry Grape-Nuts taste like wood shavings, I couldn't keep it up. I'd push myself so hard I'd get sick and my body would collapse. Or an unexpected event would throw me off my regime of restriction and I'd go flying in the other direction. Eat doughnuts and chocolate-covered raisins for breakfast, lunch, and dinner. Spend eighty dollars on a blouse I didn't want. The binge or splurge would evoke the core identity of being damaged, and I'd be thrown back into my familiar self: *I've blown it again. Now I'll never be loved. Now I'll never be worthy. My mother was right. I am a damaged human being.* Then I'd repent by dieting or returning everything I'd bought (becoming a financial bulimic). The diet/budget–binge/splurge cycle would repeat itself.

But just because human development requires the formation of an identity doesn't mean that that's who we actually are. It's possible to step back from our ongoing version of events and question the feelings, the memories, the belief systems, the entrenched and completely convincing worldviews that have developed over a lifetime. Most of the time we are so wedded to our particular perspective that we believe that the way we see things is the way they actually are. And that anyone would feel the way we do, given what's going on in our life, our finances, our body.

When you begin questioning your version of life as you see it, it's as if you step out of a pitch-black movie theater and realize it's still light outside and there's a vivid world unfolding here, now. You realize that it's possible to question the drama of your thoughts and feelings, that you are not a helpless observer being dragged by a bus along the ruts and rocks of your life.

One of the by-products of this kind of inquiry is that you can no longer blame other people for the way your life has turned out. Not because you don't want to—blame is so convenient, so cleansing, so momentarily thrilling—but because you now understand that it really isn't someone else's fault.

This inquiry process is like waking yourself up from a trance, like extricating yourself from the sticky fabric of your past. It requires wanting to live another way than the slog of life as you know it. And sensing that freedom from acting out your conditioning is possible. Also—here's the rub— being willing to be uncomfortable while the unsticking happens because it's so much more familiar, and therefore comfortable to stay the same and refuse to change.

As you become curious about your thoughts and feelings, you begin to identify with the one who is curious rather than the one who is drowning in hopelessness or sorrow or the feeling of not having enough. You identify with awareness itself. You become willing to question, say, the feeling of inner poverty. You ask yourself where it is located in your body and if it has a texture, a shape, a worldview, while simultaneously experiencing that if it is possible to question anything, then you are bigger than the feeling or pattern you are questioning. While exploring the feeling itself, you realize that it developed from the past, and that it was only an interpretation based on how you saw things then. And while this is happening, you simultaneously become aware of the space in which the patterns, the beliefs, the feelings are taking place. You become aware of awareness itself, which is a bit like becoming aware of the sun instead of the objects that it shines on. Through the questioning process, your sense of yourself as not having enough or being unworthy softens, becomes transparent, shifts. You arrive in the present moment. (For a more detailed description of this process—how to do it, the questions to ask yourself, and the stages you encounter—see the Inquiry Addendum of *Women Food and God*).

• • • • •

Along with questioning our familiar stories about ourselves, we also need to question how we see the world—and the meaning of money itself: money-learned behavior, money messages, cultural attitudes, class biases, privilege and the lack of it. Each of us was deeply affected by how our parents or caretakers handled money. We felt the tension or the yearning or the anxiety about money. We heard the fights, witnessed the humiliation, bore the brunt of the depression or the scarcity or the manipulation around money.

In school, we absorbed cultural beliefs, class beliefs, and a slew of biases. We developed a particular orientation toward money and made certain decisions about it that determine how we think about and use it today. And just as our default identity is unconscious, so too are core decisions about money. To change our behavior, we have to be aware of what is driving it. There is no other way.

My uncle Ralph told me that his father wrote down every penny he spent. They'd go to a grocery store and he'd take out a pen and paper and write the amount down. Then they'd go to the cleaners, the butcher, and his father did the same thing all over again. Although Ralph adored his father, he thought he was a penny-pincher, a tight-ass. He vowed never to write things down, never to keep track of his money. He and my aunt have gone bankrupt once and spent all their savings twice. Now they are in their eighties and have no savings, no retirement money, no cushion.

My earliest impressions about money were that it caused fighting, bitterness, hatred. When I ask my mother about this, when I say, "Mom, what was money like between you and Dad in the early years, when I was in kindergarten and grade school?" she says, "We were always scrambling. Dad worked two jobs seven days a week. Eventually, he graduated from law school, worked his way up the corporate ladder, and after that, he was expansive and always happy to spend money on you and your brother. When we had enough money to hire a decorator, the trouble started."

I don't feel that men getting angry at interior-decorating expenses is an indication of dysfunction, since my hero, Abraham Lincoln, was furious at Mary for redecorating during their first year in the White House. Although he was not prone to outbursts, he called the new furnishings she bought "flubdubs." If our first poet president, our glorious, illuminated, brilliant president, got angry when Mary exceeded her decorating budget, then what was Bernie Roth—a poor schlump from the Bronx—supposed to do?

Which reminds me of something, and excuse me if I digress for a moment, but this is important. We all know that Madoff's first name is Bernie. Now you know, because I just mentioned it, that Bernie was my father's name. And we all know that Madoff's wife's name is Ruth. But what you don't know—and I only recently made the connection—is that Bernie and Ruth are also *my* parents' names. I'm not sure what that means, but I know it's a missing link to seriously erratic behavior on my part. It's like having aberrant DNA, like being born with a missing gene, like having Bonnie and Clyde for parents.

In my conversation with Ruth the First, my mother, to discover if there is a difference between our memories of the past, I say: "Mom, did you feel that Dad was generous with money?"

"Well, not exactly. I had a lot of credit cards and could spend anything I wanted in stores, but I never had money in my wallet. And then, of course the day of reckoning would come, by which I mean the bills. And I'd go through that song-and-dance routine. Begging. Pleading. Sucking up."

During that conversation, I remembered—and felt again—that there was always a cost to having money: the loss of integrity, heart, love. By the time I was old enough to understand the money dynamic between my parents, I knew that my mother actively hated my father and yet was willing to spend his money and humiliate herself. But she also, by her own admission, used money as a weapon. We'd meet for dinner and she'd park in a $250 no-parking zone and look him in the eyes and say, "Tough." Or he'd give her a diamond ring for their anniversary and instead of handing it to her, he'd throw it in her face and walk away. When they got divorced, he shamed her in front of the store owners she'd been shopping with for years by cutting off her credit without telling her. Now that I think of it, Bonnie and Clyde might have been an upgrade in the parental nomenclature department.

To have money, my father lied, stole, and cheated. So did my mother. The goal was to have as much money as possible, and if you had to give up integrity, self-respect, compassion, and love, well, so what? At least you amassed a fine collection of antique watches. Money was the ultimate goal, but it was also tainted with sleaziness, and in my mind, having it meant being sleazy.

My default sense of self—feeling that I was bad and needed to try hard to redeem myself—became laminated to what I saw happening in my family about money and forged a relationship with money—and food, of course—based on hiding, shame, and greed. If I was bad and money was bad, and if I wanted to be loved or accepted, then I needed to hide the (bad) money I made while simultaneously trying to get more.

We all receive cultural messages about money, depending on our environments: Money doesn't grow on trees. Money can't buy happiness, but it lets you choose your own form of misery. Money is power. Money corrupts. You can't be too thin or too rich. Money talks. You can marry more in a minute than you can make in a lifetime. I've been rich and I've been poor and rich is better.

My retreat students often talk about the "suffering club"—the group of friends who bond with one another through their weight-loss struggles. They gather at lunch or at work, and the main topic of discussion is the latest, greatest diet and the diet blunders they've recently made, how they gained five pounds during their vacation or ate an entire chocolate cake the night before. If a person in the group begins to lose weight, everyone wants to know how she did it. If she loses five pounds, she's still a member of the club. Ten pounds, twenty pounds, and she is now a threat. She's not suffering anymore, and since the club is based on wanting to be, but never actually getting, thin, she's broken the "rules"—and lost her friends (or the people she thought were her friends) in the process.

The same is true with money. People gather in prosperity clubs, talk about the law of attraction, buy endless books on becoming overnight millionaires, but their underlying beliefs about money persist. Without deeply understanding the roots of our discomfort—the way we see ourselves, the feelings and beliefs we are expressing that are based on outdated interpretations of our past—we will revert to the same behavior over and over again. We will lose the same twenty or fifty pounds and gain it back for the next twenty or fifty years. We will put ourselves on budgets and read a slew of brilliant financial books, and although we might have a few months or even years of clarity, we will eventually devolve to our familiar patterns—and continue to want more money while often feeling bitterness and a teeny bit of hatred toward those people who have it.

Until we name, question, and understand our core beliefs, until we no longer feel like the victim of our circumstances and can actually inquire into the melodramas of our lives, all the good advice in the world is as valuable as my Madoff account on the day of his confession. We will always be loyal to what we believe is the truth, even if what we believe is a sham. When children are beaten or abused by their parents, they cling to their abusers' necks; they don't want to give up the possibility that one day, these same people will beam love on their sweet heads. None of us parts from our beliefs without first questioning them. We don't want to risk being separated from where we believe love is located.

Still, and perhaps most important, the point of questioning our relationships with food and money is not to be loved or thin or rich; it is not even to be happy or unapologetically ourselves. We use the core beliefs and feelings and decisions and our seemingly inexplicable behavior as portals. We use material substances—food and money—as a path to being unruffled. Openhearted. Peaceful. To contacting that which doesn't get destroyed during periods of loss or gain. Because in the end, we have to let go of it all: the money, the thin thighs, the houses, the clothes. And all we are left with is our minds and our ability to live in and with ourselves. Karlfried Graf Von Dürckheim wrote that "only to the extent that a person exposes herself over and over again to annihilation, can that which is indestructible be found." It seems that nothing real ever dies. This is a good thing.

5

Stealing Pleasure

For as long as I can remember, I treated money the same way I treated food: as if it were stolen.

When I was anorexic, I'd wait until my next-door neighbor left for work, creep into his house, take a fistful of his granola, run back to my cabin, and with heart pounding and mind racing, stuff it into my mouth. I stole it not because I couldn't afford to buy it myself but because granola was not part of my raw-food-150-calories-a-day starvation diet. I stole it because granola was one of my favorite foods, and stealing it was better than not having it at all.

But when something is stolen, whether it's literally stolen, like the granola, or shot through with a forbidden quality, you can't relax. Stolen goods are never yours—they're forever marked by how you acquired them—and so you never really own them. When you believe you need to steal pleasure in any form, you become a thief of your own desires. You live your life believing that the only way to get what you want is to steal it.

Sometimes, during a retreat I am teaching, I notice what's on a student's plate: three pieces of bread slathered with butter, a huge helping of rice and potatoes, and I'll ask if that's what she really wants or whether the bread is like stolen goods. Since no one who is not starving truly wants half a loaf of bread at one sitting, the answer is usually the latter. It's as if what I call "the Big Mother in the Sky" turned her back for a moment, during which time my student piled the food on her plate. But since she believes eating is forbidden, she has to get as much as she can before the Big Mother catches her and realizes that she's breaking the rules.

In the months following the Madoff debacle, I began to see that, for me, money was like the granola from my neighbor's kitchen. I tried to get rid of it quickly, spent it on things I didn't particularly want, stashed it in places that were out of my sight. It's not that I didn't worry about having enough of it or agonize about whether our money would last through retirement and old age. I was always fretting and calculating; I was forever comparing what we had to what we could have or would have or would never have.

My basic attitude about money was the same as my attitude about food when I was gaining and losing ten pounds a week. I want it, but I'm not allowed to have it, and if I do get it, I must hide it quickly. It's as if I were trying to build a skyscraper of a life on a sandy, shifting, damaged sense of self.

When my father died and I received a check for ten thousand dollars from his life insurance policy, I put it into my Madoff account that same day. When I got an advance on a book I sold, the money went to Madoff before I had a chance to consider whether it would be better to pay down our mortgage or lend the money to a friend to start a business. Even though we had more money than 99 percent of the world, even though there was virtually no chance that we were going to starve or be homeless, I treated our money as if it were stolen.

When I broke free from the obsession with food, I began by neutralizing the charge I'd given to it; I allowed myself to eat what I wanted when I was hungry. If I wanted coffee ice cream at eight in the morning, if I wanted pizza at midnight or Ring Dings for dinner, I allowed myself to eat them. And I gave myself a set of guidelines to follow: Every time I ate, I sat down, paid close attention to the taste of the food, and stopped when I'd had enough. The combination of legalizing what I'd considered stolen food and training myself to notice the smell, texture, and taste of what I was eating allowed food to become what it is: nourishment, sustenance, pleasure.

And I'm discovering that the same process of asking and allowing is true in the relationship with money. When I'm seized by the need to have or buy something, I'm beginning to slow down, bring myself back to the present moment, and ask myself what I actually want—which is different from what I think I shouldn't have because it's wrong, greedy. When I take the charge away, a sweater loses its enchantment and becomes just another woolly thing. Taking away the stolen quality also takes away the focus on I-me-mine. It widens the vision, allows me to see that the world is bigger than this particular thing at this particular moment. I begin to ask questions that are impossible to consider when I am convinced the only way to get something is to "steal" it. Questions like *Does this sweater/bouquet of flowers/T-shirt come from a country that employs child labor? Does the production of it hurt the environment in any way? Am I supporting something I believe in by making this purchase?*

When I first take my students through the analogous process with food by asking them what they really want, they list all the foods they believe they're not supposed to have. I point out that having what they're not supposed to have is not the same as having what their bodies want; rebellion is the other side of compliance but is not freedom. Then we begin the process of discovering what they truly want when they are not trying to prove to their mothers, who are often dead, that they're allowed to eat Krispy Kreme doughnuts for breakfast.

"Tell me the financial equivalent of eating Krispy Kreme doughnuts for breakfast," I say to my retreat students.

The answers are: "Buying gadgets I don't need," "Another jacket to add to my collection," "An iPad," "More books," "Anything that doesn't really fit my needs right now," "Anything I don't use or truly want," "Anything that gives me an instant high but is disconnected from my real values."

Before we can be aware of what we really want, the stolen quality of our relationship to money needs to be understood. You can't be shamed into being conscious. It's not the Krispy Kreme doughnuts we want; it's not another pair of shoes; it's what we think those things will give us. In working with thousands of people about their physical, emotional, and spiritual hungers, I keep hearing the same thing: Everyone wants to love and be loved, to belong, to be happy. We want beauty and joy and community. It turns out that the focus on me-me-me getting more-more-more leaves us empty-handed and poverty stricken. Because even if we have ten million dollars but are starving for joy or contact or well-being, we are members of the living dead.

One of my students writes:

> I worked on my checkbook again tonight, planning out the month. Maybe, I shouldn't try to pay off the whole credit card right now. Yes, it will cost more in interest, but it makes me so nervous to try to cut things so close. And if I fail which I so often do, I end up spending more because I just give up. Can I be kinder with myself, go slowly, making small changes over time with awareness and compassion and being in the present as I have done with food over the past four years? Can I actually let myself have (i.e., appreciate) even a tiny fraction of what I already have instead of feeling guilty about having so much—and then buying more?

Maybe I do have the capacity to have a more "normal" relationship with money, not fraught with impulsive, compulsive, and guilt-ridden decisions with each spending splurge. Maybe the relationship with money can have balance and pleasure and nourishment. I have never even considered that this was an option.

Indeed.

STORING FOR THE HUNGER TO COME

For as long as I can remember, I felt like a survivalist who moved to the desert, set up house in underground tunnels, and stocked up on three thousand packages of freeze-dried lentils for the moment disaster struck and caught everyone else by surprise. Anticipating the catastrophe before it happened seemed like my only chance at surviving in a world that was perpetually on the brink of extinction.

In my catastrophe-is-imminent frame of mind, I didn't question whether the equivalent of living on freeze-dried lentils when the rest of the world was dead made any sense. I didn't question the benefit of stocking up on ruffled shawls when there was no money to buy food. Thinking rationally and being entrenched in deprivation mode did not go hand in hand.

For one thing, when a catastrophe occurs, it is never the one you anticipated. During the ten years we invested our money with Bernie Madoff, I imagined many financial end-of-the-world scenarios: Madoff having a heart attack and no longer being well enough to continue his brilliant operation; Madoff making a few bad decisions in the stock market and the value of our portfolio going down by 30 percent, 40 percent, 60 percent; either Matt or I having a Christopher Reeve–type accident (although neither of us rode horses) or one of us needing to fly to Germany to have our blood cleansed—for reasons I cannot now recall—and needing to spend every last dollar on medical treatments. Not one of my financial-catastrophe-is-imminent scenarios included the possibility that Madoff was a fraud of epic proportions.

Another thing about disasters is that they never go as planned. When the Big One—the 1989 northern California earthquake—occurred, I had walking pneumonia, but since I was also having a bad hair day, I was getting a cute haircut on the third floor of a rickety building in San Francisco; instead of being in bed or huddling under my solid oak desk with my cat and husband, I was ducking under mirrored counters lined with bottles of black hair dye that were skittering across the floor as the entire building bucked and rocked.

My teacher Jeanne once told me that I spent the first fifty years of my life protecting myself from losses that had already happened. As if living with hypervigilance in the present could protect me from the assorted addictions, abuses, and abandonments that populated my early years on the planet. When I was eating three pizzas instead of one, hiding Mrs.

Shapiro's butter cookies under my bed, or buying three pairs of boots at a time, I was convinced I was preparing myself for the future, when I'd be bereft of sweetness or money or comfort, but since nothing I've prepared myself for has ever happened the way I thought it would, it seems that I was preparing myself for events that happened half a century ago—sort of like a modern-day Miss Havisham, preparing herself at eighty years old for the fiancé who walked out on her when she was twenty.

When we eat together at my retreats, I watch some of my students begin the end-of-the-meal windup: They shove food in their mouths, their pockets, their purses just as we are finishing. The food is going away and, even if they are full, there's an instinctive clutch, an unspoken panic, a desperate attempt to make it last, as if they were preparing themselves for the onrush of future and unbearable hunger. And even though our next meal is in a few hours, and even though there is virtually no chance they will go hungry until then—there are plates of fruit available at all times—the default famine mode kicks in, as if they were bears about to go into winter hibernation or hunter-gatherers who have suddenly come upon a wild panther and must extract every last drop of marrow from the bones before the inevitable starvation begins.

It's as if we look at the world from an old imprint—which becomes an expectation—of disaster. No matter what we have, it is never enough, because something terrible is about to happen and we are about to be left with no love, no food, no comfort. As if having money—like having shortbread cookies in yellow tins or shelves lined with sweaters—could protect us from desolation.

This is an age-old inclination, of course. Protect. Hoard. Defend. The enemy is lurking, waiting to eat you, annihilate you. Our reptilian brain, despite being augmented by the limbic brain and the neocortex, is still focused on physical survival. Fight or flight. When we allow our basest impulses—the very ones that helped the earliest two-legged beings survive—to direct the higher brain centers, we act like snakes. And given that we were born with the inclination to do whatever is needed to survive, we need to respect the genius of a brain that has done its job and brought us this far. But we also need to update our wiring, since the chances of being eaten by a dinosaur are slim. Hoarding our resources has now become maladaptive, not only because it causes us to live in a constant state of tension, which is unhealthy and therefore counterproductive to our survival but also because it promotes greed and dishonesty, which eventually lead to gross inequality between classes and eventually to economic breakdown. Also, we are fast running out of planetary resources, and soon there will be nothing left to hoard or kill.

When you store either food or money for the hunger to come, you live in a ghost world, fighting ghost demons, storing ghost food, spending ghost money. Nothing you do or eat or buy is relevant because it's motivated by the past that already happened or the future that hasn't yet come. You live without living, die without having truly landed on this earth.

The impact and meaning of a catastrophe are not in the event itself. The ability to tolerate it is a function not of what happens but of our relationship to ourselves and our own minds. In that simple realization is absolute freedom.

• • • • •

We can store for the hunger to come; we can live as if catastrophe were imminent. We can hide and sneak and stuff food, shoes, dresses; we can pretend that it's possible to protect ourselves from the big horrible thing. Or we can wake up.

My friend Ruby, a single mother and Madoff investor, says:

> I know this sounds like a minor thing to focus on after losing all the money I'd saved for twenty years, but I can't stop thinking about a candle I bought. Usually, I am so focused on saving and scrimping, but for some reason, about a year before Bernie Madoff confessed, I bought an outrageously gorgeous candle. I spent thirty dollars on it and promised myself weekly that I was going to light it, that I was going to use it, that I was going to really enjoy it, but I never did because I was saving it for the right time.
>
> Now, post-Madoff, I can't even describe the grief I'm in. My days are spent crying; I can barely function. When I think about the nights—year after year—that

I worked late and didn't get to read my daughter a story, when I think about everything that I put off until I could save enough to start my own business, I feel like I am going to break apart with grief. All that money is gone. But so are the nights I spent making it. So is my daughter's childhood. It was like I was starving myself daily for the feast that was going to come, except it never did.

Losing that time with my daughter is worse than losing my money. Burning that candle, like being home instead of working in the evenings, was a luxury I couldn't allow myself. Now that my daughter is grown and my money is gone, I'd like to think I learned something about not postponing what I love in the present for a future that may never come. I'd like to think that I'll burn that candle really soon, but I don't know if I will.

As Ruby and I talk, I am aware that the mistake I kept making without realizing it was assuming that what I wanted most could be stored. Saving/storing money is useful. Making sure that we have enough to eat is important. But when it becomes a substitute for a certain kind of intimacy or aliveness, it's no longer about the substance; it's about the ways we deaden ourselves, re-create our pasts, protect ourselves from losses that already happened.

The big horrible thing isn't the plane crash or the earthquake or the diagnosis. When those things occur, we act, we know what to do. We live or we die. Hell is what we do in the meantime. It is the ways we starve our souls as we prepare for the future that never comes as planned. The true disaster is living the life in your mind and missing the one in front of you.

6

Free Money and Other Fabulous Myths

My work with compulsive eating is built around a set of seven eating guidelines, most of which address hunger and satisfaction. A few of the others, however, are directed at related issues like sneaking, allowing yourself to have pleasure, and distracted eating. Two guidelines in particular—"Eat sitting down in a calm environment; this does not include the car" and "Eat without distractions"—have elicited copious tomato-throwing indignation over the years.

The reason for this is that we compulsive eaters, like compulsive spenders, like to do the deed under the radar, pretending that the apple pie in the grocery basket is for the kids, not for us, or that the money we just spent on a new coat, despite not needing a coat, is utterly justified because it was on sale. According to this unique way of calculating finances, we actually saved, not spent, money.

When I describe the two aforementioned eating guidelines to an audience, I'll often say that together they could be called "Ways We Eat Without Eating" or "Free Eating for All." Then I ask for examples.

Here is some of what I've heard over the years:

- Edging a cake. If I walk by a cake every few hours and take the teeniest "slice" off an edge, I'm not eating it; I'm evening it out so that it looks pretty.
- Broken cookies. When the cookies break, the calories break.
- Before exercise. I'm about to burn it off, so it doesn't count.
- Illness eating. My body needs the food to get better.
- When my mother-in-law comes to visit. It's obvious. I need to fortify myself.
- Off someone else's plate. I'm just tasting.
- On my way to or from the stove/refrigerator/table. They're just scraps, dontcha know.
- Standing at the refrigerator. I'm grazing, not eating.

The it-doesn't-count myth also shows up in the way we think about and spend money. I was walking down a Manhattan sidewalk with my friend Lulu a few nights ago when she found a twenty-dollar bill. When, after five minutes, no one seemed to be looking or coming back for lost money, Lulu said, "Yippee! Found money! Let's go buy hot fudge sundaes."

Lulu is a single mother who works at a ten-hour-a-day job and struggles to pay her bills. Still, there was something about found money that removed it from the category of *money* money—the kind that costs something to make. As if the two thousand cents in the bill she found had a different value from other bills of the same value. As if, as a single mother, she couldn't use that money to buy food for herself and her child.

More examples of ways we spend money that don't count:

- When something is supposed to cost ten dollars and it costs five: "Now I can buy two!"
- When we amortize the expense: "These earrings cost fifty dollars, it's true, but if I wear them every day for the next year, they cost 7.3 cents a day. At less than a dime a day, I can't afford not to buy them!"
- When someone else is buying. "Well, I might not really need it, and really, I don't even like it, but why not take it anyway? It's free."
- When we've won the money in a bet, in the slot machines, or by gambling.
- When we inherit money and there is a lack of connection between the money and the energy it took to make it. After my friend Amanda received a surprise check from her mother's estate recently, she told me that her first response was that it was free money. "I hadn't counted on it to pay the bills or

the mortgage; I felt as if I could spend it on stuff I wouldn't have ordinarily bought."

Since the value of a dollar bill is the same no matter how you get it, our various ideas about free money are not about the money. They are all ways we rationalize doing what we want to do anyway. And there's nothing wrong with this; it's not good or bad. But it is helpful to know ourselves well enough to understand that when we say that edging a cake doesn't count or that money we make at the slot machines is free, it's our minds we're describing, not money: *I want to binge, so I'm finding a way to do it. I want to gamble, so I'm finding a way to make that acceptable.* The upshot here is not about shame or judgment; it's about awareness. It's about freeing yourself on a daily basis so that you don't ever have to hide behind your own back. It's about choosing to eat that piece of cake or buy that coat without having to twist yourself into odd little shapes to do it.

But it's also about having the freedom *not* to eat the cake or buy the coat. As long as you are rationalizing about why it's okay, you are rebelling against the voice that tells you that it's not okay.

I want it. You're not supposed to have it. I want it. No, you shouldn't. Go to hell, I deserve it.

Once you understand the battle that is really going on, you realize that the swing between having and not having is code for your beliefs and that your behavior is their outermost expression. Unless you question the beliefs upon which your actions are based, the actions will continue.

One of our main (and usually unspoken) beliefs is that it is only through shame, judgment, and deprivation that we truly change; we are convinced that if we allowed ourselves to know or have what we really want, we'd end up broke and fat. We are also convinced that if other people knew the truth about our desires and the way we act them out, they'd be horrified—and so we sneak and lie about what we want most. But the problem with repressing desires is that instead of going away, they get stronger. When you tell yourself to stop thinking about a polka-dot poodle, you see polka-dot poodles in your kitchen, your favorite chair, everywhere.

One of my students writes: "I keep trying to force my body into shape and to come up with a budget and a plan to reach my goals of 'financial freedom.' And then I rebel, because whenever I count calories or exercise to lose weight or try to restrict the money I spend on food, clothes, travel, etc., I always end up eating more or spending more and enjoying it a lot less. I understand more than ever that I can't find freedom by fighting myself."

Rather than engage in the usual fear tactics of repression, it's possible to make room for wants and desires. The contemporary Indian sage Sri Nisargadatta wrote, "The problem is not desire. It's that your desires are too small." Instead of acting them out or being afraid of them, it's possible to use what you think you want—chocolate, silver filigree earrings, to be fabulously wealthy or incredibly thin—as a doorway to what you truly want. Although bittersweet chocolate is, it's true, a daily necessity, if you find yourself wanting huge amounts of it, you can use it as a signal, a portal to desires of which you might not be aware: the desire to be more vulnerable, the desire for meaning, the desire for more sweetness in your life.

A student named Annie says, "I buy and buy because I want a piece of beauty for myself." I ask her about that desire. Who doesn't love beauty? Who doesn't want a piece of it for herself? As we explore the desire, she sees that she is assuming that the beauty is out there and she doesn't have it. It makes sense that if she is convinced that the only way to have what she needs is to buy it, she will keep buying. When she stops fighting the need for it, she begins to question the assumption that beauty is only out there, not anywhere in herself. She begins to relax, and slowly, through this inquiry process, she begins to see how she formed her beliefs and why she has, until now, assumed they are true.

Because she is not frantically trying to either repress her need or act it out by spending money, she begins to feel herself from the inside out, which is in itself both satisfying and beautiful. Beauty, she sees, is not located in only one place. It's over there, but it's also here. It's subjective; it changes; it answers a particular need on a particular day. In this moment, which is all she has, her relationship to beauty has changed.

The next time she is seized with a need for beauty, I tell

her, we'll go through the process again. And again. For as long as it takes, because what better thing is there to do with our time here on earth? Through the process of inquiry and treating yourself with curiosity and kindness, you use what you believe is worst about you to discover what is best about you.

THE WHAT-THE-HELL MYTH

I decide every week—on Mondays, the same day I used to decide that I was going to diet—that I am going to restrict my spending. Then I buy something I wasn't expecting to buy and I feel such despair that I run up even more credit-card debt, which makes me feel so much more despair that I have to buy myself something else to feel better.

—A retreat student

Lord, give me chastity and continence—but not yet.

—St. Augustine

Oh, what the hell. I've already blown this week's budget; I might as well buy that new microwave too. What the hell. I told myself I would diet, but I ate that carrot cake, so I might as well eat the gallon of ice cream as well. What the hell, we've already spent so much money on this vacation, we might as well spend more. I want to diet, I want to budget, but not yet.

The what-the-hell myth comes from the mind that believes in black or white with no in-between. If we've blown it a little, we might as well blow it all the way. If we eat a bite, we might as well eat the entire thing. If we've bought a pair of shoes, we might as well buy the purse, the stockings, the skirt that goes with them. It's a mind-set left over from being children who haven't yet learned to hold the tension of opposites (or that the mommies they worship can also be mean and tired—and that that doesn't mean the end of the love as they've known it). In this black-or-white thinking, you're either good or you're bad, you're right or you're wrong. One wrong move and you're off the deep end.

While it's tempting to feel powerless (because there's always the hope that someone big and powerful might save us), it leaves us shipwrecked in the land of despair. *I can't do this. It's too hard. What's the use? I'll always be fat and broke and in debt. Why try? What the hell.* A retreat student named Jamaica writes, "I don't ever see myself as having a stable financial environment. I still live very much like a child spending all her birthday money or allowance because what's the use of saving it. There's nothing learned, nothing saved. And then I think, what the hell, I don't have a lot of money to spend, so I might as well not clean my house, eat junk in front of the TV, wear ratty clothes. No money + unhealthy weight = unworthy. But I deal with my situations like an ostrich with its head in the sand. Then I wonder each time why it hasn't changed and the behaviors and anger and frustration start all over again."

Ouch.

Like free money, the what-the-hell myth is a way we interpret our experience, a way we laminate our beliefs onto reality. It's also another way to justify having what we think we want—as much as possible, no reins, no limits—instead of exploring what we actually want. (See the If-Only-I-Had Myth for more on this.) But since the interpretation is self-created, we can uncreate it through awareness. Is it really true that because you bought that coat you should also buy the shoes, purse, and skirt? Is it true that one move off your declared path makes you a loser? That being ten pounds over your natural weight makes you unworthy? One of my students writes, "I remind myself over and over again to be aware of this breath, this moment, this step. Like a mantra, it brings me out of the scary stories. There is peace even in the middle of all the pain. This is the real magic, the real fairy dust, the mythical truth—all I ever longed for is mine, right here, now, always."

THE IF-ONLY-I-HAD MYTH

If being rich made people happy, all rich people would be happy. If being thin made people happy, all thin people would be ecstatic. And although we've all read the stories of the lottery winners who are abjectly miserable, and the rich and very thin celebrities who cycle among making movies, taking drugs, and being in rehab, we persist in the myth that more money and less weight leads to more happiness. And although most of us weren't over-the-moon happy when we lost weight those previous ten or twenty times or when we had more money than we have now, we keep the myth alive, as if the alternative—not putting our lives on hold and living here, now, in this moment, with all that we have and don't have—were intolerable. We've become so acclimated to the if-only–I-had myth that we don't bother to question it. Has being thin ever, in one single instance, made anyone happy? If it made you so happy, why did you gain the weight back? Do you know one rich person who is happy because they are rich? Is it really true that the way things are now is intolerable?

We live in a trance; we make up the stories we tell ourselves, and then we act as if those stories were true. We create a make-believe world with make-believe assumptions, putting our real lives on hold for a make-believe life that has no relation to our direct experience.

Let me be clear: It's not that losing weight doesn't make us more comfortable if we are huffing and puffing when we schlep our bodies around, and it's not that having enough money to buy food and shelter and clothing and basic comforts doesn't make life easier. I'm not disavowing the importance of living in a body that can get around with ease or having enough money for basic comfort. But when we begin ignoring what we do have, we miss the only place that is real, the only place from which we can glean any kind of happiness or satisfaction or love—which is here, now. And if we haven't learned how to see through our myths, quiet our minds, and be in the present moment, it doesn't matter if we are thin or rich; we will do what we've always done: raise the proverbial bar and miss the ongoing feast that is now.

A few years ago I was in a car accident in which I ended up in a wheelchair for a few months; after the first few days of being dazed and in shock, I realized I'd been handed a temporary gift: Since I couldn't walk, move, or think clearly, I had the luxury of not being able to do anything—and being "forced" to notice the throbbing, teeming, knock-out beauty of "nothing." Sometimes, as Matt would be wheeling me around, the phone would ring and he'd leave me facing a wall. Since my ribs were bruised and I couldn't navigate the wheelchair by myself, I'd end up staring at the wall for five minutes, ten minutes. And after silently cursing him for a few seconds, I'd relax. *Oh,* I'd think*, there's no place to go and nothing to do. I don't have some big important task to accomplish today; I don't have to* be *anyone today. It's just me and the wall.* And then, either because I was on mind-altering pain medication or because I could no longer think of "here" as a way to get "there"—or anywhere—I could see what I'd been missing on my way there: everything. Because, as Gertrude Stein said, there was no there there. Before the accident, even when I got where I thought I wanted to be, even when I reached my goal, there would be a new goal, something I didn't have.

The only place you can feel love is here, now. The only time you can be aware of your humanness or the generosity of other people or the courage of a friend is right now. The only place you can taste the crisp bite of an apple is here. Now. When we pierce the trance—or something pierces it for us, like a death or accident or financial loss—it's as if we step out of the dream and into the crystalline freshness of life itself.

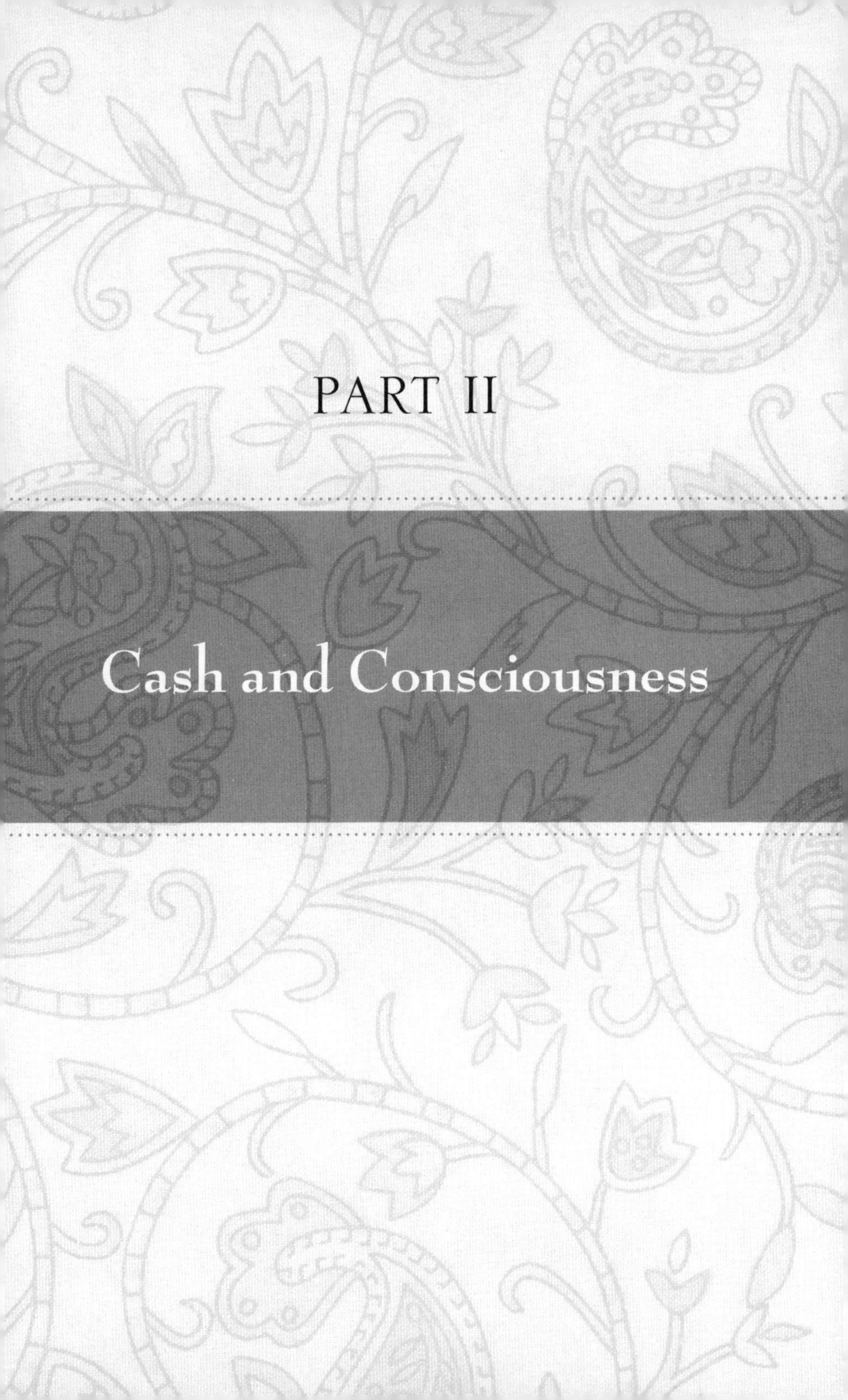

PART II

Cash and Consciousness

7

Being Saved and Saving

Over a spicy eggplant dinner at a Thai restaurant, and as part of my new hobby of interrogating everyone I encounter about intimate details of their financial lives, I asked a friend of a friend, who also happened to be a Madoff investor, what had changed since the day in December when Madoff confessed. "I've swung into high gear," she said. "I restarted my occupational therapy practice, I started putting some old jewelry on eBay, and I am constantly scheming about how to earn more."

"And your relationship to money? Has that changed?" I asked.

"Huh?" she said. "If you're asking whether I feel pissed off at Madoff, if you're asking if I've forgiven him, if you've asking whether I've taken this as some kind of spiritual lesson, the answers are: I'm pissed, I haven't forgiven him, and no. And

I'm especially furious at the culture we're living in and the fact that it encourages everyone to want more and more and more. My house is leveraged to the hilt, I owe the bank hundreds of thousands of dollars for a home equity loan, and I'm pissed that I have to deal with this at this point in my life. I'm sixty-five years old, it's time to let up a little, not work harder."

"Do you feel any responsibility for what you're describing?" I asked.

"Look," she said impatiently, "I grew up as an upper-middle-class WASP in the suburbs of Boston. Although my father said, 'Money doesn't grow on trees,' it didn't feel that way. I had an ever-increasing supply of whatever I wanted. Now I have less than my parents did, and my kids will get even less. And I'm pissed about that. It doesn't seem fair. I keep hoping that something wonderful will happen, that I'll have another big win."

Six years ago, she and her husband invested in Google before it went public—and they hit the jackpot: Their initial investment grew to two million dollars. Then they lost half of it in a real estate fiasco, invested big in Madoff, lost big in Madoff. "A few months before Madoff confessed, we invested money in another IPO that sounds fantastic," she said. "Now we have a chance for another miracle, another big win."

Me too, I thought, *I'd like a miracle. I want a fairy godperson too.*

Oh, that's right. I've already had three: Bernie the First, my father (lied about his will; did jail time; read further in this chapter for the sordid details); our close friend and accountant, Louis Izarro (embezzled our money; did jail time); Bernie the Second (stole our money; will die in jail).

I don't seem to have a knack for picking financial saviors. And therein lies the pickle: When you have a savior, you don't have to be accountable for your present circumstances because the future—when everything that is wrong will be right and an abundance of love, work, and money will be yours—is right around the corner. Having a savior—which can also translate to participating in the next get-rich-quick scheme (or the newest diet)—allows you to remain a child.

My friend Rosie said, "When you ask about my finances, it feels like you are asking about everything I've never wanted to think about. And as soon as I realize that wow, I'm an adult, I need to think about this, need to take some responsibility here, I realize that taking care of my financial situation means I have to stop living in the fantasy that I'll get everything I never got as a kid. That I'll finally have the perfect mother or father." Or, as Anne Lamott says, being an adult is "like baby-sitting in the Twilight Zone. I keep waiting for the parents to come home because we are out of chips and diet-coke." And while I realize that waiting for the adults to come home—even if you are eighty years old—is a natural human tendency, it is especially prominent in the relationship with money.

From a retreat student:

> Just as my relationship to food is an expression of my fantasy of wanting someone to give me unconditional,

totally devoted love (as opposed to taking care of myself), my relationship with money fuels the fantasy of being taken care of by someone I deem bigger and better than myself. If I couldn't have my mother's love (because of her depression, prescription drug use, and eating disorder), then at least I could have my father's money. And at forty-six, I am still holding on to the fantasy that there will always be someone there to take care of me. I work hard, I started my own business, I am a single mother supporting two children. But I still spend money believing that I will always have more coming, despite the knowledge that there really isn't any more coming. And the ironic thing is, I don't have much to show for all the money I spend. I spend it with such irreverence that I am having trouble paying for repairs I need in my home.

Speaking of fathers. When my father was diagnosed with stage-four lymphoma, my brother Howard insisted on seeing a copy of his will. Howard did not believe my father's promise that the three million dollars he'd recently made in the stock market after his company went bankrupt was divided 50–25–25 among my stepmother, my brother, and me. "Show us the will," Howard said to my father. "Let us see for ourselves."

I never doubted my father, not for a minute, and I was embarrassed that my brother did. Every time he'd bring up the will with my father, I'd try to creep out of the room, to show my father that it wasn't me who needed proof. For as long as I could remember, my father had been my lifeline, my hero, my redeemer. The problem was that loving my father also meant diminishing myself. Being loyal to my father meant being loyal to the contract between us: He was the big one, the smart one, the one who knew about money and finances and work. And I was his ditzy, blond cohort, although I was smart enough to know that being loved by him meant not contradicting his version of himself.

As I got older and noticed his dishonesty or insensitivity, I'd stiffen my body and intentionally distract myself, refusing to let facts or feelings destroy my relationship with the person who tethered me to life. By the time my brother questioned my father about his will, I was so good at not seeing what I saw, feeling what I felt, or knowing what I knew that I could have been sitting with Hannibal Lecter and convinced myself that he was Albus Dumbledore instead.

Being saved implies staying small and willfully blind. But it also implies one more thing: Since not everyone can be saved, the saved one must be imbued with something different, something extraordinary. To be saved, you must invest in being special. You must cling to the belief that you deserve to be saved and other people—siblings, friends, strangers—the poor schmoes, don't.

When Howard pressed my father about his will, he reluctantly showed us a two-page, five-and-dime document entitled

"Last Will and Testament." Sure enough, it said what he'd told us it said, and I felt vindicated. "See?" I said. "Dad would never ever do anything to hurt us. He'd never lie to us." What I didn't say was *Maybe he would do that to you, but he wouldn't do that to me. He'd stand in front of a moving train to save my life. I'm special. He'd give me anything. Of course he is leaving his money to me. And since if he leaves it to me he will also leave it to you, there's no need to be concerned. You, Howard, are protected by my orb of specialness.*

I was wrong and Howard was right.

After his death, we discovered that my father's millions were held in his retirement fund, which was not included in his will. And because he had not added an addendum to his will, the retirement money was distributed according to New York State law, which meant that his current and fourth wife received the entire sum.

In the face of so many incontrovertible facts, my denial kicked in. I told Howard that my father must not have known the law or that he must have neglected to change his will after he went bankrupt and lost the money that was included in the will he showed us. My brother reminded me that my father was an expert in probate law; he created wills and trusts for many people—and managed to break irrevocable wills and trusts for other people. If there was anything he knew, Howard said, it was New York State law. Then he reminded me that if my father was smart enough to follow the stock market every hour of every day for the last three years, know when to buy and when to sell, and make three million dollars from an initial thirty thousand, he was shrewd enough to adjust his will.

I wanted to be adored and lavished upon more than I wanted to see the man himself. Or as a friend of mine once said, "When my psychological survival is at stake, I am not interested in the truth." This lack of interest, combined with the need to be special, made me an easy target for Bernie the Second.

The relationship with money, like the relationship with food, is a way we act out beliefs that we don't know we have. Coming face-to-face with my desire to be special has meant facing its opposite: the pain, beliefs, and needs that *created* the desire. The part of me that believes it's not worth a dime. In my book *The Craggy Hole in My Heart*, a memoir about my father, I wrote that it wasn't that I wanted to be given a million dollars; I wanted to know I was worth a million dollars, to believe that my father's love was that big. I needed to be special so that I could silence the voice that told me that I was a self-indulgent, unlovable bitch. As long as I was putting my energy into proving how special I was, I never had to face the heap of ashes inside.

The truth was that I loathed myself. And even as an incredibly privileged, unbelievably successful, and happily married adult, the self-loathing endured. When spiritual teachers asked the Dalai Lama about self-hatred, he didn't understand what they meant because the feeling that we are bad, damaged, wrong is peculiarly Western—and unless we name it, lean into it, and look at the self-hatred straight on, we remain afraid of who we believe we really are. We turn our lives into endless self-improvement projects so that the badness will turn to goodness. And we remain victims who need to be saved, although the main thing from which we need saving is our own self-hatred.

Part of the process of dealing with money is understanding the hopes, the dreams, the fantasies that we've projected onto it—and debunking them one by one. When money becomes simply money—a means of exchange that allows us food, shelter, clothing, and comfort—instead of the antidote to our low opinions of ourselves, we can begin using it in ways that generate well-being rather than exacerbate insanity. But we cannot have a sane relationship with money until we have a sane relationship with ourselves.

During the years we invested with Madoff, I could not think clearly about what would happen if Madoff was a liar. To consider that possibility, I would have had to pierce the need to be special that investing with him represented. And I would have had to let go of seeing myself as a child who needed to be saved by a big, powerful father who knew more than his dumb, blond daughter. Most of all, I would have had to finally stop clinging to the fantasy that my self-hatred could be resolved by the love or the money from another human being.

Being committed to being special enough to be saved is synonymous with being committed to being unconscious. You can't be saved from yourself and be aware of the truth at the same time. The cost of remaining loyal to unconsciousness is that you remain dependent on the big, powerful daddies who are themselves unconscious—and darkness rules. If you are not willing to face that which you believe will destroy you, you will never discover that who you truly are can never be destroyed.

A Zen teacher once told me, "Leap and the net will appear." *Yeah, right,* I thought. In my own case, neither my father's lies nor our financial adviser's betrayal was enough to force me to leap; neither were my years of therapy and meditation practice. I knew that I'd interpreted my mother's involvement with drugs, men, and her own unhappiness as a sign that I was the kind of girl that even a mother couldn't love. I knew I blamed myself for her behavior because that's what children do; I'd worked with my shame at being myself for as long as I could remember. But it took losing everything I'd saved to see that I didn't need to be saved.

When we lost our savings, when I wasn't sure whether we would be homeless, it was impossible to hide behind my mantle of specialness. During those first few weeks, I felt as if everyone were laughing at me, gloating about our loss. "You think you're so special? Ha! You are finally getting what you deserve." It was as if my insides were on my outside and now everyone could see what I'd been trying to hide for fifty years. But when my friend Annie said, "You can come live with me and I'll raise you as my own," and Stephanie said, "You can come live in our house; it's small but we'll manage," and I felt an almost unbearable outpouring of kindness from strangers and students, I realized that the only hatred I was running from was my own.

When people find out I was invested with Madoff they ask if I thought I was special. If I felt as if I were getting away with something when everyone else was losing half their money. My answer is "Guilty on all counts. I wanted to be special. I wanted to be protected. I wanted to be saved."

But who doesn't?

We're all muddling around doing our imperfect best, trying to hide or improve or figure out ways to be safe, special, loved, because the alternative—exposing the dark side of our feelings, our beliefs, our impulses—feels like throwing ourselves out of a plane without a parachute. If we are fortunate, we get the props ripped out from under us sooner rather than later, or at least before we take our last breath. Because then we can find out who we are when we are not blindly reacting to our conditioned fears and feelings and beliefs.

When she was asked about the purpose of meditation, Pema Chodron said that it simulates crisis conditions in our lives so that we are able to notice and work with our deeply grooved conditioned reactions. When you have to sit quietly and watch your own thoughts, and when those thoughts are uncomfortable or frightening or dreadful, when they bring up anxiety or panic or sorrow, you have the chance (if you don't run screaming from the room) to learn what is beyond those feelings: the warmth, the compassion, the empathy, the tenderness, the utter sweetness of your heart. While your reaction may be *I'm supposed to voluntarily and artificially simulate the worst experiences of my life? Hello?* consider this: The crisis is inevitable; the Madoff investors simply got there in a hurry and in one giant leap. If it's not the economy, it will be something else, like old age, illness, and death.

As the Buddhist teacher Stephen Levine says, "Either you will die before people you love die or they will die before you. There are no other choices." So why not begin now, with what you are hiding, with your secret shame?

• • • • •

The other day, as I was standing in a grocery line, I ran into yet another Madoff investor—his name was Martin—and asked him how his relationship with money had been going since the loss. "Not so well," he answered. "I feel like a bad Buddhist, even though I've been practicing for forty years. There is no way I can make what happened okay. I'm seventy years old; I lost everything; I have to go back to work at a bookstore, which doesn't look like it will be around for much longer. I feel enraged and ashamed and at a complete loss of what to do or where to go from here."

"What about those feelings makes you a bad Buddhist?" I asked as we inched toward the cash register. I was very interested in this because of the many judgments I've had about myself: that I am a bad meditator, that I am a spiritual failure, that if there really is a judgment day when we die, I'm going to get left back a grade or go to hell.

Martin said, "The anger, the shame, the depression. I should have been able to deal with these. I should have been bigger than the feelings."

My apples, bananas, and butternut squash began to move forward on the black conveyor belt. The cashier started to weigh them, ring them up. I turned to the bad Buddhist and said, "Take it from me, who has done the same thing to herself over and over: The Buddha, I am certain, would be incredibly unhappy to hear that you are feeling shame about your shame."

The bad Buddhist stiffened. "I regret to point this out, but you have no idea what the Buddha would say."

He's wrong, though. Because although I am not exactly a religious scholar, I know that any true wisdom tradition or religion is about being fully human. Reggie Ray, a Buddhist teacher and scholar, writes that "spirituality is not something that can in any way be separated from human life itself; in a very real sense, the spiritual journey and human existence are one and the same." And although I wouldn't believe the Buddha just because he said so, I have experienced this over and over and over again, beginning with my relationship with food. When I stopped waiting for the genie to appear and make me thin tomorrow, when I refused to go on one more miracle diet that would take off thirty pounds in thirty days and began to name and be curious about what I believed were the most awful, shameful parts of myself, those very behaviors led me to a freedom and exhilaration I'd never imagined possible. And the very same thing is happening with money.

There is nothing special about wanting to be special. Nothing special about shame or loss or anger. The real specialness lies in the willingness to turn toward it instead of hiding from or reacting to it. To let yourself fully understand the extent to which you've rejected your own humanness. The problem with wanting to be special or saved is not the desire itself; it's that you believe yourself and stop your inquiry there. You think the miracle is out there, in another person or a thinner body or a shower of hundred-dollar bills. In an attempt to hide what you consider shameful, you believe you need to be saved from yourself without realizing that everything, even the desire to be special, is part of this existence and is therefore included in the blessing.

It's right here, in this very body. Your particular life, with your particular feelings and behaviors and desires and quirks, is the very definition of specialness. The holiness is closer than your own skin.

8

Giving and Receiving

At the end of the second night of a post-Madoff retreat I am teaching I ask my students to bring cash to the morning session—from one to five dollars.

"Did you say cash?" someone says. "We're supposed to bring *money* to the meditation hall?"

"Yup," I say.

"It feels wrong," someone else says, "like letting the money lenders into the temple." Heads nod; a wave of murmurs courses through the room.

I point out that we haven't done anything yet, that just *thinking* about money has created a stir. "Let's find out more about this," I say. "Bring your money in the morning."

They look at me suspiciously as they file out of the room.

• • • • •

At 10:00 A.M., they arrive at the meditation hall with money in hand. Some are carrying five-dollar bills. Some have their hands stuffed with ones. A few are toting a single dollar bill. One woman says, "Did anyone forget their money? Because I have extra."

"In a few minutes," I say, "I am going to ask you to mill around the room carrying your money in your hands. When you are face-to-face with another person, you are either going to give or receive money. If you're the giver, decide whether you want to give some or all of your money away, at which point you will say, "Here. I'd like you to have this." If you are the receiver, you are going to take the money and say, "Thank you. I appreciate it." Then you are going to continue milling again. When you come face-to-face with your next partner, you are going to go through the whole process again: deciding whether you are the giver or receiver, deciding how much money you want to give, giving it away, and receiving what is given. You are going to say the same things—'Here. I'd like you to have this,' 'Thank you. I appreciate it'—and move on. At some point, in about three minutes, I will ask you to stop and sit down. Any questions?"

"How are we supposed to decide whether to give or receive?"

"One of you will have an impulse to act first and follow through on the action."

"What if we end up with more than we started with?"

"You can either keep the money you end up with or we can give all the money to the scholarship fund for the retreat," I say. "But before we actually do the exercise, I'd like you to imagine that the exercise is over and you're back in your seats. Tell me about the cash you have in your hands at the end: Is it more or less than what you started with?"

A thirty-year-old named Catherine says, "I will end up with less because I have to. I will feel terrible if I end up with more than I started with. In fact, I will feel terrible if I end up with more than anyone else."

"Is that how you feel in your day-to-day life?" I ask.

"Absolutely," she says. "If I have money, I make sure to get rid of it quickly. It's like that saying about burning a hole in my pocket. I don't feel as if it's okay to have a lot—and it drives my partner crazy. I'm always giving money away, jewelry away. I gave away my favorite earrings last month to someone who said she liked them. It's like something terrible will happen if I have too much, so I always make sure I don't."

Mia, a real estate broker from Miami, says, "I imagine that I will end up with more money than I started with. I imagine that I will end up with *a lot* of money, at least twenty dollars. But then, as soon as I imagine that, I know it's not true. I know that I am someone who never ends up with the good stuff. I feel doomed. Like something in me is damaged or bad and it keeps showing up in everything I do, including the amount of money I have."

I ask one after another of my students what they will have at the end of the exercise.

"I will end up with more than I started with, and I will feel terrible about that, but not terrible enough to do anything about it."

"I will end up with nothing, and then I will feel needy and small and begin figuring out how to manipulate other people to get more."

"I will walk around the room pretending that I am nice and want to give some money away, but in my heart I will know that I don't give a shit and all I want is to keep what I have and get more."

"I'll have a lot more than I started with, and I'll feel better than all the suckers who ended up with less. As if it means something about me that I have more money than they do. As if that makes me a better person."

"I am going to end up with exactly what I started with because I don't want to give any of it away. And if I have to, I will make damned sure I get it back. Fair is fair."

"I already feel bad that I didn't bring enough. Even though you asked us to bring from one to five dollars, I should have brought ten."

"I could lie right now, but the truth is that I believe that no matter what I ended up with, it wouldn't be enough. I've never had enough, and even if I ended up with all the money in this entire room—which is what, really? four hundred dollars?—it wouldn't be enough. I feel like a bottomless pit."

"Money is sleazy, dirty, and it makes people do odd things. I hate having this cash in my hand, hate having to do this. Why can't we just go back to meditating and focusing on food?"

I notice one of my longtime students, a woman named Marion, walking to the back of the room during this discussion as she nonchalantly stuffs money into her bra. No one can see her but me, since they are all looking toward the front of the room, but since this too is part of the pattern we are exploring, I imagine that Marion believes she has no other choice and that she will speak about this later.

"Okay, everyone, be aware of the way you usually see yourself and your relationship with money. Now, let's start the milling part of the game."

Although I've never done this exercise myself—Matt and I brainstormed it together the night before the retreat began—he did an exercise like it at a presentation he gave before the Madoff debacle. Matt asked everyone in the audience to take out from one to ten dollars. Some people didn't have any money, so he asked those of us who did to give some to those who didn't. I wasn't pleased with this request. Matt had gone over his talk with me the evening before, but he'd never mentioned this exercise. *Why the hell didn't he?* I thought, because as the wife of the presenter, I felt obligated to make sure everyone could participate in the game, which meant taking dollar after dollar out of my wallet. At the thirty-dollar mark, I closed the wallet and began sending my husband dirty looks.

Matt did an imitation of James Brown's "I Feel Good" and asked everyone to throw their money up in the air—and leave it on the floor. At the end of his talk, he said that people could either pick up the money they had brought or leave it for the local homeless shelter, whatever the group decided.

(Note: The point of this exercise, in Matt's talk, was to give him a chance to sing a James Brown song and to give everyone a chance to have fun. That's it. You can probably understand why I decided to stop teaching with him years ago. Matt would come out and everyone would jump around and laugh. I'd come out and say, "Laughter is good. Laughter is healing. Now let's look at what's going on beneath the laughter." The audience wanted Matt back.) When everyone began filing out of the room and I was certain no one was looking, I picked up twenty of my thirty dollars. Within a few minutes, I was standing alone in the room with a pile of cash in my hand. I felt like that guy in the *Twilight Zone* episode who had a watch that stopped time. He used the watch to rob a bank. He pressed the button and everyone turned to stone. He walked into the bank, opened the cash drawers, took out piles of money. On his way out of the bank, he dropped and shattered the watch. Then he was left with millions of dollars, alone in a world where everyone and everything was made of stone—and there was no way to go back. Like him, I cared more about the cash than the people. Because two years later I was still ironing out the kinks between money and me, I figured I could be a compassionate witness for my students.

• • • • •

Eighty women begin walking around the room, and the inevitable exchanges begin. The energy is charged, noisy, pulsing with excitement. I watch as a new student named Victoria scuttles to the side of the room and tucks a few dollars away in her backpack; another student runs to her wallet and takes out more cash. At the three-minute mark, I ask everyone to stop, sit down, notice what happened and how they feel.

Catherine says, "It ended up just as I thought it would: I have less than anyone else, less than I started with. I can breathe again. This is why I keep eating. Because food is the only thing that I give myself, that I allow myself to have a lot of."

Another woman says, "I am ending up with nothing, not one dollar—and I feel bad. But I feel good about feeling bad. Like Catherine, if I had more than other people, I'd feel bad in a different way. I'd feel guilty and selfish. And I'd rather feel bad about not having enough than feel bad about having too much."

"I want more," Beth says. "I know I shouldn't want more, but I do. And the same thing happens with food. No matter what I have, I want more. It's like there is an empty place inside me and no matter what I have, it's never enough."

"I ended up with more than I started with and I feel antsy, like I have to give it away quickly. It's what I do with my money in real life. I have it but can't hold on to it—I fritter it away on expensive things that, when all is said and done, are meaningless to me."

As we talked about what happened during the exercise, it was apparent that their beliefs about money, although incredibly charged, were expressions of what they believed they were allowed or not allowed to have in the rest of their lives. With food, with friends, with family. And their beliefs seemed to largely determine their experience. Their predictions about what would happen during the exercise were almost exact descriptions of what actually happened.

My teacher Jeanne says, and I've quoted her often, "We all follow life instructions given to us ten or thirty or fifty years ago by people we wouldn't ask street directions from today." We absorb a set of beliefs before we are old enough to think for ourselves, and unless we question them, they become the default lenses through which we enter into every situation we encounter. "Don't be so full of yourself; people don't like that" can eventually, if we hear it in multiple situations, become the belief that "if I want to be loved and accepted, I need to dumb myself down." If we see our parents arguing about money, if money is a source of conflict in our families, or if no one ever talks about it, we give meaning to those situations in the form of beliefs: "If I want to be happy in a relationship, I'd better not think about, not talk about, not bring up the subject of money."

According to psychiatrist David Krueger, author of *The Secret Language of Money*, we understand situations by giving them meaning. And the meaning we give them is in the creation of beliefs—which, once formed, become the template for how we see ourselves and how we behave. We then spend the rest of our lives acting as if our subjective beliefs—*I am dumb/lazy/unlovable, I will never have enough, Money corrupts, Rich women are bitchy*—were reality itself. We believe that the way we see our situations is the Way Things Are; there is no other way. And our actions proceed accordingly.

Most of us don't even know what we believe; we are so convinced of the rightness of what we see and feel that we don't realize that we see things as *we* are, not as they are. It never occurs to us that our belief system is subjective, that there are dozens of ways to interpret the same situation, and unless we name and recognize the extent to which our own version of reality is based on instructions given to us by people we wouldn't ask for street directions today, our emotional, financial, and spiritual lives will remain frozen in the past, hijacked by beliefs that, for the most part, are out of alignment with, and have no relevance to, our current ideals and values and the adults we've become.

It is impossible to replace one set of beliefs with another by only using what the New Age movement has labeled "affirmations." You can repeat "I am lovable" a thousand times a day, you can put "I am successful beyond my wildest dreams" on your mirror, your computer, your dashboard, you can sing it to yourself when you go to sleep and think about it the minute you open your eyes, but if an earlier belief or conviction of being unlovable is installed in your psyche, you will be wasting your time because you won't believe yourself. If you don't do the actual work of deconstructing your fundamental beliefs, the affirmations have no place to land or stick; they won't work.

It wasn't until we lost our savings that I first understood what I believed about money. I watched my father lie, cheat, and steal. I watched my mother spend outrageous amounts of money to get back at my father. I saw how he used money to wield power over my mother, my brother, and me. I felt humiliated by my desire to have his love, get his money, and stockpile things. Without realizing it, I interpreted what I saw and fell into a core money belief.

Although each of us has many and, to some extent, conflicting money beliefs, my main one was that it was impossible to have money and be kind, be loving, care about anyone but oneself. So when I started making money, I was in an unconscious bind. To like myself, to maintain a semblance of self-worth, I couldn't have what I had; I couldn't have money. But since I didn't know this, since I hadn't named or questioned it, the belief led to a series of actions and nonactions: I refused to think about the money I made. I kept pushing it out of sight and into my Madoff account; I abdicated any responsibility or accountability for making and having money. While diversification sounded good, I would have had to see myself as someone who had enough money to take the necessary actions to diversify. And I couldn't. I wouldn't.

But I was also acting on another core and seemingly conflicting money belief: that there wasn't—and would never be—enough. Enough love, enough money, enough rest, enough food. The frenzied hunger for more was part of the air I breathed as a child, and I did a valiant job of carrying on the pattern as an adult. I ricocheted from believing that money was dirty, sleazy, politically and spiritually incorrect, and I had to get rid of it to believing that no matter how much money I had, it wasn't enough (so I'd better keep it in Madoff, where the returns were good).

Was that greed? Absolutely. It was greed born of the family I grew up in, the culture I live in, and my refusal to wake up from my own delusions masquerading as beliefs.

When people say things like "Your beliefs determine your experience; therefore, if you believe in being poor or if you believe you deserve a new house that's what you'll get," they are interpreting a basic law of the universe—that when you look through shattered lenses, the world looks shattered—on a superficial and materialistic level. It has always been true that you act according to your beliefs and, since the way you act has consequences, your beliefs manifest in the world through various situations. When you act out your beliefs, you see the results of your actions everywhere.

Does that mean that everyone who invested in Madoff believed that money was sleazy? That we all were driven by the belief that there would never be enough or the unconscious desire to be relieved of our life savings? I can't answer for everyone; I have a hard enough time answering for myself.

• • • • •

After we did the money exercise at my retreat, I called out the beginnings of sentences and asked my students to call out the first ending that occurred to them; I wanted to reveal the underpinnings of our money beliefs. Here are the results:

Rich women are . . . bitchy, thin, checked out, shallow, privileged, selfish, uppity, sparkling, distant, mean, different from me, difficult, free, spoiled, lazy, unconcerned with the environment, good dressers, lucky, insolent, brassy, overconfident, arrogant, thin, more like men.

In my family money meant . . . power, begging, secrets, everything, nothing useful, disagreements, lying, suffocating, getting by, selfishness, misery, hard work, trouble, shame, giving myself away, other people, food on the table, going without, not caring about other people, love, good shoes.

Having a problem with money allows me to . . . be helpless, be worried, hide, be safe, not have to risk, stay small, be liked by everyone, be with my mom, have something to look forward to, be numb, be good, keep suffering, put my life on hold until I am rich, be broken, be ashamed, be the same as everyone else, focus on more spiritual concerns, feel politically correct.

If I didn't have a problem with money, other people would . . . hate me, not want to be with me, be jealous of me, expect more of me, not believe me, belittle me, want to be with me for the wrong reasons, borrow from me, not see me, want me to take care of them, be proud of me, be hard to get rid of.

If I had money, I wouldn't be able to . . . bitch, have excuses, complain, fantasize, worry, feel poor, postpone my life, feel limited, be myself, be the victim, concentrate on myself, make excuses, stay self-righteous, ask for help, look sad, be the martyr, say I'm not good with money, be broken.

Money is . . . dirty, sleazy, the reason the earth is ruined, responsible for all that's wrong, cheap, incompatible with spirituality, the tool of the oppressors, for other people, what movie stars make a lot of, not for me.

One thing I do with both food and money is . . . not know what's enough, not let myself really have them, numb, restrict, ignore consequences, overindulge, feel like they're out of my hands, endlessly imagine what my life will be like when I am thin and rich.

My "normal" is . . . miserable, broken, depressed, dramatic, neglected, flawed, hurried, not good enough, an improvement project I call my life.

At the end of the sentence completions, we sat in silence for a few minutes. The evidence was apparent: If we believe that having money means not being able to ask for help, if money is the reason the earth is ruined, if rich women are checked out, uppity, spoiled, and difficult—and if the situations in our lives are the ways we act out our beliefs—it makes sense that we would avoid having or thinking about money with any degree of clarity and discernment. We might avoid taking actions (paying off our debt, not using credit cards, researching ways to use our money that are in alignment with what we care about most) that would result in a cogent relationship with money. To some part of the unconscious mind, avoiding dealing with money translates to avoiding falling into the traps of being bitchy, selfish, unconcerned about the environment. It allows us to avoid being cast out, being envied, being lonely. And if being screwed up about money for the rest of our lives is the "cost" we pay for being part of the tribe, well, so what?

Clearly it is taking different actions, not just naming beliefs, that leads to change, but in my experience with both food and money, achieving long-lasting change is impossible without first becoming aware of the deep-seated convictions that are driving your behavior. If you don't realize that the way you are seeing things is not the way they are, if you don't understand that you see yourself, your family, your relationships with food, money, and the world through a version of reality that you developed before you could talk, you are like the embryo in the Rumi poem who, when told that the world outside "is vast and intricate. / There are wheat fields and mountain passes / and orchards in bloom," says, "There is no 'other world' / I only know what I have experienced. / You must be hallucinating."

• • • • •

Before Bernie the Second confessed and went parading around in that tacky quilted jacket with the collar turned up and got pushed around by the reporters, I knew I was "hallucinating" about my relationship with money, but I didn't care. I felt like my retreat student Gloria, who said, "I work so hard in the rest of my life that I feel like I deserve an easy path with food—a long, smooth glide to the other side." Ditto. I was tired. My thighs and eyelids were going the way of gravity, I'd written books, taught hundreds of workshops, gone all the way with food. Someone else needed to figure out money. I wanted to keep buying pretty things, giving chunks of money away to animal and earth preservation, and racking up interest on the money I'd invested. Being honest with myself about my beliefs about money—and the behavior that expressed them—seemed like opening the proverbial can of worms. There was too much shame, greed, and pain associated with money. Also, I didn't want to see anything that would force me to give up buying more sweaters or bangles.

But with the shock of losing our money, the veils ripped between worlds and I glimpsed another way of living. I saw what enough was. Tasted freedom from the need to acquire. Realized that my relationship with money was divorced from that in which I professed to believe: selflessness, consciousness, community—and that another way was possible, even though I didn't know what that meant on a daily basis.

For me, the change happens slowly, daily, decision by decision. Every time I don't walk into a store, every time I decide not to go for the quick buck, every time I pay with cash, every time I realize that what I am buying has consequences to other people. Once the light gets switched on, the possibilities are endless, exhilarating. Wheat fields and mountain passes are everywhere. Orchards are in bloom. Even at this late stage, with all that we've destroyed, anything is possible.

9

Enough Isn't a Quantity

My father was not a passionate man except about things; he could sit through an entire meal without speaking, drive in a car for hours without saying a word. But when he'd buy a new watch to add to his budding collection, gladness would rearrange his face and spread like a summer day to the blue table, the shag carpet, and me. Another watch! And such a beauty! Isn't it a fabulous day, an incredible life?

For a few hours after his purchase, he'd burble around the house. "Would you like to go to Bloomingdale's?" he'd ask. "Is there anything you want?"

I'm not sure when I began cashing in on my father's largesse, not sure when I gave up wanting what I really wanted and decided instead to grab what I could get. I only know that by the time I was eleven, I stopped longing for my father's attention and love for their own sake and learned how to use them as commodities I could trade: a watch for him, a pair of shoes for me. A watch for him, a necklace for me. And once I made that turn—once I accepted the act of substituting things for human contact—having enough of anything became impossible.

Hostess Sno Balls, which I've probably written about more than the Hostess company itself, were my favorite childhood treat; besides being pink, my favorite color, they were also cheap (ten cents a package). One day when I was twelve, I walked past my parents' bedroom and heard my brother crying. "I bought two Hostess Sno Balls, one for me and one for Geneen, and you ate them both," he blurted. My father, who could eat a dozen Fig Newtons in thirty seconds, laughed and said, "I don't remember eating them, but I probably did, and I am sorry." I skulked into my room without saying a word, since I knew that it wasn't my father who had eaten them. I'd scarfed them down the day before without a thought about my brother. The fact that my brother had thought about me—that he had actually wanted to share with me—made me feel selfish and guilty and ashamed because it wasn't the same for me: I didn't care what he wanted. I didn't care what he needed. I didn't have enough to give away. It was as if I were shot full of holes and my next step depended on filling them. But since the fillings didn't touch the holes, I kept going back for more.

As a child, it was more food; as I got older, it was just more. More clothes, more friends, more love. More recognition, more furniture, more boots. More money. I had to have more because I believed that I was less—and I didn't want anyone to know. I wanted to be seen as nice, generous, loving; I was certain if anyone knew the truth—that I was so intent on filling myself up that I didn't care who I hurt in the process—I'd be cast out of the tribe. So I spent my time acquiring and accumulating and stockpiling while trying my best to look sweet and kind and giving.

The nub of any addiction is the belief in your own deficiency and the assumption that it can be fixed by a tangible substance. A woman I know from college binges on twenty, thirty, forty thousand calories a day, day after day, for weeks, months, years. She eats until she is so full her stomach hurts, her organs ache. She is nauseated. She is bloated and burping and farting. The next day she wakes up and does it again. Eventually she stops. Then starts again. Year after year, for twenty years, she has been doing the same thing. It's not about the food. She binges on almond butter, green vegetables, fruit, leafy greens. It's not about the weight. She is slim, wraithlike. It's not about the money. She has a million dollars in her bank account. It's about the holes that food can't fill.

A student named Kimberly has 196 pairs of shoes. I ask her if she wears them all. "Yes," she says, "I do."

"Do you like them all?"

"Yes, she says, I do." I don't ask why she needs—or wants—196 pairs of shoes. There is no answer to that. It is the same as asking someone who is bingeing on a carton of ice cream and is already full why she keeps eating. It is the same as asking a person who has five or twenty million dollars why they feel driven to make more. *Because I am trying to feed something that can't be fed. Because I don't know what else to do or where else to turn. Because I am forty years old and the dreams I had didn't come true and the possibilities are narrowing. Because at least buying shoes or making money gives me something to do.*

A money manager tells me that he's never met an ultra-wealthy person who believes they have enough money. "If they have three million, they want six. If they have twenty million, they want thirty. If they have a billion dollars, they want two billion. Years ago a man came to me with six hundred thousand dollars to invest," he says. "He told me that if he had three million, he could relax. He wouldn't worry. When we reached the three million mark, he said he needed five million. I understood then that no amount would ever be enough."

If you're trying to fill something that can't be filled with what you're using, the emptiness never goes away and you keep wanting more.

It seems that being human comes with an inherent developmental quirk: Every one of us believes that something is fundamentally wrong with us. Buddhist teacher Tara Brach calls it "the trance of unworthiness." Diamond Approach teacher Hameed Ali says, "We believe we were born with a stain, with a defect, with a flaw, and it makes us feel we are bad." He says that since no child grows up in a perfect environment, each of us sensed correctly that something really was wrong: the lack of attunement to our needs. We internalize that preverbal discomfort as the belief that "something is wrong with me" and spend the rest of our lives haunted by and ashamed of the deficiency that we believe is unique to us—and trying to hide and fill it.

Once my teacher Jeanne asked me what I really wanted when I wanted to buy yet a third pair of UGGs. "It's not what I want now," I said. "It's what I wanted then." And since one of my main spiritual practices is inquiry—being curious about my experience rather than trying to fix or change it—I could relax into the deprivation and scarcity of what I didn't get then and discover one more time that when I allow the lack to be there, there is no fight, no shame, no desperate need to fill it.

I have been practicing inquiry for almost twenty years, and there are times when it still feels counterintuitive to me. Relax into deprivation? Feel the extent of the lack here, now? Yuck. But after the initial resistance, there is always the moment when the identification with the past-as-me dissolves and I no longer believe the story I am telling myself. As soon as I stop fighting the deprivation, I realize that it's in the past and that what I really wanted then—what the hole formed around—was a feeling, not a thing. I wanted to know that I mattered. And because there is no shame in that—every child wants to know that they matter—there is a surge of tenderness for my parents and their desperation and for me and mine. As the deprivation dissolves into tenderness, I have now what I wanted then: the feeling that I mattered. There is no hole, no frantic need for UGGs.

Although I have been saying this same thing in a thousand

different ways since I wrote my first book, it seems that the process of unwinding the contractions in our souls needs to be experienced over and over. At some point, we become willing to see that what prompts the desire for more (chocolate, boots, money, gas, oil, land) is the trance of deficiency—and that trances don't disappear with more stuff.

When I ask my students about feeling deficient and having enough, they say:

> I felt most "broke" when I was married to a high-earning doctor from a wealthy family and when I lived with my upper-middle-class dad as a child. No matter how much I had, there was a nagging feeling that who I was and what I had was never enough.

> I own a flourishing business with all kinds of opportunities to increase my revenue. I buy about 60 percent of what I want and 100 percent of what I need. But on the inside I never feel safe, full, rich, wealthy, good enough, loved. It's like the feeling of "not enough" is programmed into my cells.

> I get myself in trouble, and it is usually with used-car–salesmen types that I can't stand up to, because deep down inside I agree with them. No matter what they are trying to sell me—wrinkle cream, diet pills, a cell phone, or a new leash for my dog—I agree with them

that I need it, and more importantly I can't afford it. That makes me a loser. That makes me angry, and I want it all the more for spite, to show them I'm good enough.

It's almost impossible to think about other people/countries/the earth, to consider what you are destroying, when you are convinced that your survival depends on getting more. When you believe that you deserve to have whatever it is, that it's not fair that you got so little, and that you don't have enough of what you need, your heart develops a crust and that crust keeps you separate, isolated, and alone. You feel guilty about your selfishness, you feel ashamed that you are not as generous as you could be, but you also feel defensive and protective and self-righteous. *I need this. I have to have this. I deserve this. I don't have enough.* Under the spell of deficiency, we can justify anything.

In *The Soul of Money*, global activist Lynne Twist writes, "Sufficiency isn't two steps away from poverty or more than enough. Sufficiency isn't an amount at all. It is an experience, a knowing that there is enough, and that we are enough. It is consciousness about the way we think about our circumstances: making known to ourselves the power and presence of our existing resources and our inner resources. If we look around us and within ourselves, we will find what we need. There is always enough."

Over tea with Lynne, I ask how, in her understanding, people evolve from believing in their own deficiency to seeing what they already have. She says that sometimes events do that for us. She says that she's worked with people whose children have died and they suddenly realize how much they love their partners. Or who lose their homes and realize how grateful they are to be alive. Or who lose their money to Bernie Madoff.

In the first ten days of December 2008, Matt and I had more money than most people in the world and I didn't believe we had enough. On December 12, we had nothing, and after the first few days of feeling devastated, I knew what enough was because, for the first time in my life, I had it.

Before we lost our money to Madoff, I'd been complaining about our house. Built as a vacation house in 1960, it was drafty and cold, and the plumbing didn't work. We sometimes had to take showers outside, even on fifteen-degree winter days. After Madoff confessed, I couldn't believe my good fortune to have a house for that day and the day after, even if we might not be able to keep it.

Before Madoff confessed, I didn't like the way Matt chewed his cereal, wore ankle socks, was insistent on focusing on the positive. After Madoff confessed, it seemed miraculous that I'd ended up married for more than twenty years to a man I adored. I remembered again how much I liked his face, his laugh, his walk, the way he rolled his eyes.

Before Madoff confessed, I'd peer at my life from the holes in my psyche. I looked at myself and saw the emptiness of the eight-year-old with the sagging neck of a fifty-six-year-old. After Madoff, I was grateful to have a body, hair, eyes, legs that functioned.

Optimists get on my nerves, and I've never counted myself in their club. I'm not a person who believes that things work out for the best; lemonade from lemons is not my style. I don't believe in angels or in the God that most people call God or that justice always comes around. I believe in disaster, that everything that can go wrong will, and that I'll end up lonely and fat with moles on my chin that have bristly hairs sticking out. So it is a bit out of character that losing every penny from thirty years of life savings did not send me spiraling into depression or hysteria or Paxil.

But even I couldn't ignore the obvious: I'd spent years saving for a future that was never coming to protect myself from a past that had already happened. I'd been convinced I didn't have enough when I had more than a million dollars. And the money I'd thought I had I didn't actually have because Bernie Madoff stole it the second we opened our first account. Ten years of statements and positive returns and dozens of hours calculating what we would someday do with what we would someday have—all of it was based on a lie.

When you are suddenly confronted with having nothing and you realize that you once had a million dollars and treated it as if it *were* nothing, you see that the very beliefs on which you construct your life are totally, 100 percent of the time, in your head and have nothing to do with reality. If I could believe that we didn't have enough when we did and then lose it and believe that we did have enough—what or where is enough?

If it really was something out there—a definable quantity—

then everyone who had that quantity would know they had enough. And since we know that's not true—the anorexics believe they are too fat, the ultrawealthy believe they need more money—we also know that enough can't be out there. Enough cannot be in something we can touch or buy or have like money or a thin body or UGG boots. Enough isn't an amount; it's a relationship to what you already have. But each of us has to find this out for ourselves.

If anyone had told me before Madoff confessed that we had enough, I wouldn't have believed them. And because, alas, it is too late to have your money stolen by Bernie Madoff, the discovery of sufficiency needs to be an inner passage that always starts with being aware of the exact place you avoid: your perceived lack.

You do this not to drown in lack or lock it in place, although that is often how it feels when you stop fighting with it. You name and sense the lack because you need to see what you truly believe before you can change it. As long as you are contracted and ashamed and guilty about needing more, you will try to hide your shame from yourself and other people. You will grab and shove and take because there isn't enough, and if life is like that game of musical chairs, if someone has to be left without a place to sit, it's not going to be you.

And this is why: Beliefs and thoughts lead to feelings, and feelings lead to actions. Or else feelings lead to beliefs, which then lead to actions. We respond to other people, treat our children, mates, strangers, coworkers based on our beliefs;

everything we do, every word that we utter, every relationship we have is an expression of what we believe.

The belief that I am not—and don't have—enough might manifest in feeling desperate for more, which might manifest in eating too much, shopping too much, investing with people who promise me a big return. My belief that I don't have enough will make me utterly blind to, and entirely callous about, those who have less because I believe that I am one of them; when I am caught in the trance of deficiency, my job, my only job, is to do whatever it takes to get more. If fortune throws a million dollars in my lap (as fortune did), I won't see it. I won't believe I have it. I will find a way to make it disappear so that the world I live in will be congruent with my beliefs. In dozens of experiments examining everything from voter preferences to gorillas marching across basketball courts, scientists have discovered that we don't believe what we see but see what we believe.

Until I am willing to name my beliefs, either because circumstances force my hand or because I wake up to the pain of seeing through distorted lenses, I will continue to act on my fantasy version of reality, which is why lottery winners blow through their cash and end up broke; even with tens of millions they believe they are poor, and actions always conform to beliefs. And I will continue to believe that my version of reality is the way it is, not the way I choose it to be based on my beliefs.

Naming beliefs and working through the feelings that cluster around them is an ongoing process. Once, in an attempt to work with my shame about the Sno Ball syndrome—wanting it all for myself—I saw a therapist who said to me, "Pick something in this room that you like." I looked around and chose a beautiful desk clock with gold filigree.

"Great," she said as she picked it up and held it in her lap. "Now tell me what you like about it—and then ask me to give it to you."

I wanted to leave immediately. "No way," I said. "I'm not asking you to give that to me."

"Two minutes," she said. "We'll stop in two minutes. Let's see what's making you so uncomfortable."

"I like the delicate numbers," I finally muttered, thinking that this was a ridiculous game, and I was furious at the person who recommended the therapist to me. "Will you give it to me?"

"I'm so glad you like it," she said, "but it's mine, and I like it too. You hold it if you like, but you can't have it. It's mine."

"You're not allowed to say that," I said before I knew what I was saying.

"Why not?" she asked.

"Because it's wrong."

As I sat there, I flipped through years of memories—the moment in the brown velvet bedroom when my mother told me she was getting a divorce from my father and told me I was selfish for crying about it, the year she gave my cousin Laura a jacket she'd promised to me and was furious at me for being sad about it. One memory after another, each charged with my same interpretation: It was shameful to want what I wanted, feel what I felt, and be who I was. And it was especially wrong to have anything for myself.

The therapist said, "Being able to say, 'It's mine and you can't have it,' is a developmental necessity. If between the ages of two and four a child is not given permission to feel and say that, if a parent does not defend a child's right to have what's hers—including her feelings—but instead tells her that she has to share or that she's selfish, that same kid will grow up not being able to be generous. How can you give away what you're not supposed to have?"

"That sounds like New Age fluff to me," I responded, although the part of me that had never gotten past being two years old was shouting, "Wa-hoo! The truth comes out!"

"And anyway," I said to the therapist, "what's the remedy? To go around acting like a two-year-old and saying, 'It's mine. It's mine and you can't have it' "?

"No," she said, "the remedy is to allow yourself to truly have what you have. And to enjoy it without feeling shame or guilt."

. . . . .

To the extent that I believe I'm not supposed to have it, or that I need to give it away now, I walk around feeling like I don't have enough no matter what I have. And even after directly experiencing sufficiency post-Madoff, I still slip into the old deficient skin I recognize as me. I convince myself I need another pair, more money, the biggest piece. Sometimes the deficiency is centered not around things but around who I am. I feel less than, unworthy, stupid. I shouldn't be writing this book. I shouldn't have written any book. And each time, with each descent, the process is the same: to name and question the core belief or contraction. To be willing to feel what I most want to avoid and to ask myself if what I believe is true now, in this moment. There is a difference between deficiency and self-hatred. Deficiency is a feeling of lack and emptiness. Self-hatred is aggression turned against yourself.

There are no shortcuts, no ways to conjure up positive visions of sufficiency and affirm your way out of your beliefs. A few months before Madoff's demise, I decided that I had too much of everything and that I needed to be more expansive and giving. I went through my closet and gave away three quarters of my clothes—twelve huge garbage bags full—to the American Cancer Society and the Salvation Army. As I was dropping the bags off, I felt so light that my body seemed to be emitting sparks. I imagined a homeless woman finding my green sweater with the fringes, a woman with breast cancer discovering my bright red waterproof boots.

A week later, I woke up in the middle of the night with my heart crashing. *Damn,* I thought. *I can't believe I gave away that black puckered coat or those gray flannel slacks. What was I thinking? I need those things. I've got to have them back NOW.*

I schlepped back into San Francisco to the American Cancer Society and sheepishly told the woman behind the counter—the one with the bandanna wrapped around her head, bald from her recent chemotherapy treatments—that I had made a mistake. I needed my clothes back. She was gracious about my request and took me to the room with mountains of clothes, and I spent hours sorting through heaps of sweaters and pants until I found my gray pants.

It was like the time I suddenly decided that I needed that pizza I'd thrown out the day before and started picking through the moldy cottage cheese in the garbage pail to retrieve it. Or the time I broke into a friend's apartment after I gave her my Weight Watchers ice cream to hide for me (so that I wouldn't binge) and decided, while she was away, that I needed it back. Since she lived on the second floor, I had to borrow a ladder, climb to her window, and pry it open. All to get ice cream that tasted like freeze-dried socks. It's hard to be curious and compassionate toward yourself when your hands are covered in moldy cottage cheese or you are taking clothes away from cancer victims. Still, since you are creating your world in every moment, with every belief, there is no other place to begin.

10

Motherlove and Fathercash

It is a Thursday night in the middle of January during my freshman year in high school, and my father is an hour late for dinner. We don't usually dine together as a family; Howard, my brother, and I eat Swanson's fried chicken TV dinners or tuna fish and Oreos, since my father works in Manhattan until midnight and my mother drinks with the martini crowd at North Shore steak house. But tonight my father said he'd be home early, so we are sitting in our dining room underneath the crystal chandelier, eating iceberg lettuce with ketchup-and-mayonnaise dressing, lamb chops, and Le Seur canned peas.

My father blasts through the door like a rocket. Without saying a word, he pulls out his silver money clip with the thick wad of bills folded neatly inside it. His eyes are glittering as he takes the pile of bills out and throws them up in the air.

"Go!" he screams. "You get to keep whatever you grab."

The three of us fall to our knees in a frenzy. My mother's long, red nails scrape the white faux marble floor. My brother laughs in high giddy barks as he picks up bill after bill. My new black fishnet stockings rip at the knee. I am frantic, intent on coming up with a fistful of cash, even if it means knocking over my mother; my father towers over us laughing like Mr. Clean in a navy blue Brooks Brothers suit.

Through the whorls of the sculptured table legs, I see flashes of my mother's blond hair, her thick knuckles, a corner of her black silk dress, the toe of one green shoe. Howard is behind me, so I can't see him, but I can feel his warm breath on my leg, hear the sound of dollar bills crunching beneath his knees. With only five twenties in my hands, I crawl nearer to my mother, convinced that the hundreds are near her. Just then, she says, "Five hundred dollars. Bingo!"

Damn.

I scan the floor; two lonely dollars are scattered near the doorway. One has a piece of lamb stuck to the corner; the other has mashed lettuce on George Washington's face, the result of our being caught in midbite when the bills like ticker tape drifted to the floor.

I get up, leaving the dollar bills where they are. Looking at my brother, I notice that he managed to snatch another hundred in various denominations. My father sits down at the table, ready to eat.

"Great game," he says, grinning broadly, "isn't it?"

Although I can only remember crawling for dollars this one time, my cousin Laura, who was in college at Long Island University at the time, told me that my father did this a handful of times—and so did we. He'd come in from work and throw the money up in the air, and those of us sitting at the table would fall to our knees and make the grab for cash. Laura said that coming up with a few twenties and an occasional hundred-dollar bill was like being on *Queen for a Day*; she got enough money in ten minutes to last an entire month at college. "I never saw anything like it," she told me recently. "It was wild. But it was worth it. That money paid my food bill, part of my rent, and sometimes I had enough left over to buy a new pair of shoes."

None of us thought it was unusual that we had to crawl on our knees while my father towered above us laughing. We learned by experience that men with money have unlimited power over those who don't.

. . . . .

When I ask my students about their relationships with food, they almost always mention their mothers. When I ask about their relationships with money, it is their fathers whose tales they tell.

> The more my father gave, the better he seemed to feel. But as I got older, I became aware of the not-so-subtle message from my father that wanting to pay for

something on my own was synonymous with rejecting him—and being rejected by him. By my twenties I was struggling with a fierce desire to be independent while simultaneously feeling entitled to not have to work for anything. And the desire for the new car, the new apartment would win over the deep belief that the dependency on my father would sink me. Later, the amounts of money got large, the gifts more extravagant—and the conflict between wanting the money and knowing I shouldn't take it continued. It is exactly like the food battle—"I want it," "I shouldn't take it," "I want it," "No, don't take it," to "Fuck it, it's mine. He wants me to have it, and who cares if I ever learn how to be responsible with money?"

At fifty years old, I am still struggling with money (and food). I act as if there's a big daddy coming to save me even though my father has been dead for twenty years, I'm divorced, and there's no man or money in sight.

My friend Janey's father was a failed businessman. "If there was one thing I learned from my mother," she says, "it was to starve myself with food. And if there was one thing I learned from my father, it's that men cannot be depended upon for financial security." When I ask how that affects her life now, she says, "I keep finding men who are as irresponsible with money as my father. And even though I swear to myself that

I am not going to rescue them like my mother rescued my father, I do. Then I end up resenting the hell out of them because they are hopeless, dependent wimps, and the relationship ends badly."

While I realize it is a gross oversimplification to associate food with mothers and money with fathers—and that there are many other factors involved in one's relationship with both food and money besides the stereotypical associations of mothers with caretaking and fathers with worldly support—it's worth pausing for a moment—or a chapter—to explore the effect that our fathers have on the way we approach financial decisions in our lives and with our partners. Because as I examine my own illustrious and disastrous monetary history, my father's prints are everywhere.

My father put his faith in anything that brought him closer to money: being cagey, being slick, putting one over on "the poor schmucks who don't have the smarts to have the big bucks." He trusted what money could buy: Cadillacs, silk ties from Talbot's, dinners at the Four Seasons. And he worshipped those who lived lavish, flamboyant material lives: businessmen, celebrities, kings. He had the buttons on his jacket sleeves moved from an inch to an inch and a half apart so that he could be just like the Duke of Windsor, whose wedding ring he eventually bought at an auction.

To my father, net worth and self-worth were synonymous, and money itself—making and understanding it—was the domain of men. To my father, women were broads, objects, carriers to transport breasts and asses. When my friend Diana—who was seventeen years older than I and eleven years younger than my father—came home with me for Thanksgiving one year, my father greeted her by pinching her ass at the airport luggage counter.

My relationship history was littered with men who were flashy, work obsessed, and not particularly interested in women as equals; choosing Matt was an anomaly. My father was a crook; Matt's father was a lawyer who represented the people the crooks like my father stole from. My mother wore five-inch heels and wasn't on friendly terms with our kitchen; Matt's mother wore Birkenstocks and was on a first-name basis with the food editor at the *New York Times*. In my world, despite the affluence of growing up as a middle-class boomer, there was no such thing as enough; in his world, despite living in a two-room apartment with two working parents, scarcity was unknown.

When Matt and I first got together, we, like many couples, never discussed money. When, after being together for five years, we began making financial choices as a couple, we chose a man that, natch, reminded me of my father.

Everything about Louis Izarro smelled like money. From his bright red Mercedes with vanity license plates—my father had a silver Mercedes with vanity plates—to his three-piece suits and Gucci shoes, Louis was lavish—and in his presence, we felt lavished upon. For the first ten years we worked with him, he only did our taxes. But then, on an ordinary summer day at a meeting at Louis's house in the wine country with lemonade in our glasses and five golden retrievers roaming around, he told us about an investment opportunity, a tech stock that had not yet gone public. "I'm only offering it to my special clients," he said, "and I want you to put everything you have into it because this is going to make you billions. If it doesn't do well, I'll give you every cent back that you put into it."

Despite my allegiance to pessimism, I was a true believer in Louis and therefore in the investment. I believed he cared about and wanted the best for us, just as I believed that my father loved me best. I was convinced that Louis was our good daddy, our reward for God knows what, since we didn't exactly have a hard life. In everything he did—the way he swaggered, the way he dressed, the way he laughed—he reminded me of my father. Someone who was looking out for me, someone who would allow me to abdicate responsibility for myself. Still, we managed to restrain ourselves and invest only a quarter of our savings with him.

A year and a half later, before the tech company went public, Louis disappeared, and we soon discovered that he'd stolen our money for his own real estate ventures, the way my father stole his clients' mortgage money to start his real estate company. Then we discovered that Louis had been stealing from us for years—the money he said he'd invested in deeds of trust that were coming due had never been deposited in the correct accounts; we'd sat with him at dinners and weddings and book celebrations and all the while he had been stealing from and lying to us, much as I'd sat with my father when he was dying as he lied to me about his will.

In the wake of the grief and loss about Louis, our close friend Richard, a successful lawyer and businessman, was indescribably kind. And because he felt so much compassion for us, he told us about an investment that his father had discovered and that he'd been in for more than twenty years. It was a safe investment, like putting your money in the bank. He said that it didn't have the highs or the lows of being in the market. It's where you put your money if you wanted to avoid scams like Louis's, he said. And although it was only open to his friends and family, he was going to include us in the group he'd organized years earlier and from which he took no percentage of profits earned. Because of his kindness and our disaster with Louis, we too could invest in a no-risk investment with a former chairman of the NASDAQ, a market maker, a veritable genius: Bernie Madoff.

• • • • •

One of the most painful things about sifting through the Louis wreckage was my pull to remain unconscious. I didn't want to know what I knew or feel what I felt; I didn't want to take one speck of responsibility for what had happened. As I ricocheted between shock and rage, I had endless conversations with Louis in my head, excoriated Matt for not being smart enough to see through him (he was the man, after all, the smart one, the one who was supposed to know), alienated friends who were clients and fans of Louis's and had encouraged us to invest with him. But the thought that I had made any contribution to our disaster felt like blaming a rape on the victim. Louis was a sociopathic liar who cheated and stole: How was that my fault?

The difference between understanding my part and blaming myself for Louis's part escaped me. The only way I knew to deal with the pain was to make it other people's fault; examining my beliefs and the behaviors that expressed them felt like taking a sledgehammer to a piece of ice that was already cracking. I couldn't ask myself why I continued in a relationship with someone who'd kept us waiting for hours before every meeting, fast-talked in language I couldn't comprehend, took weeks to produce paperwork that should have taken hours. I couldn't wonder why the fact that he wasn't a CPA or a registered financial adviser—that he wasn't anything recognizable but tall and suave and full of fancy language—hadn't alarmed me.

I forgave Louis his excesses, lies, and bravado the way I forgave my father and laughed at his Mr. Clean act of throwing money into the air. I was determined to have a man who adored me, and if his behavior did not resemble what I needed, I'd take the raw materials—face, body, breath—and create my dream father. My dream accountant. My dream investment manager, the former NASDAQ chairman.

A student named Bo writes:

> Growing up I adored my dad, was a daddy's girl, longed to be with him, and hung on his every word. But he was gone a lot, running his company and gambling. One way he showed affection was by giving me presents; it was not just the material possessions, but the excitement of the extravagance and all the possibilities it promised. Whatever I longed for showed up as reality, except, of course, more time with him. When I was little, it was baby dolls, toys, and puppies, morphing into cars and trips as I got older. No coincidence I married a man who was extravagant when we were dating—taxicabs for a couple of blocks, telegrams to say "I'm sorry," gifts from Neiman Marcus, expensive restaurants, but emotionally unavailable as he drank and drank and became an alcoholic.

The problem with remaining unconscious is that we keep creating the same patterns over and over.

From another student:

> My father was unable to earn money to support us, all the while pontificating and writing books about the misuse and abuse of money (and the power associated with it) in ecclesiastical and political arenas. As part of the white majority, he asserted we, his daughters, were "privileged," with access to acquire money that minorities didn't have. So the family money (my

> mother's inheritance) went to champion causes supporting the "marginalized and disenfranchised." Now, despite my success as a therapist, I have a hard time keeping money. I find a way to spend it or give it away, usually in the form of "loans" that never get repaid. In my practice, I let folks run a tab, unable to feel entitled or unwilling to stop the treatment until they can pay. I still see myself the way my father saw me: as part of the white majority, and so I don't take care of my basic needs. I perceive myself as "privileged" à la my father's laminate, so when others have a need, I subjugate my own needs and wants to theirs.

The patterns will endlessly repeat themselves, in our relationships with others, ourselves, money, food, until we question them. But to do that, we have to break through the inertia. We have to act.

In my own case, with no more money to lose and no ego to protect—it's almost impossible to puff yourself up when you've been taken for everything you've got—I realized I could afford to look at my beliefs and the behaviors that expressed them. And I couldn't afford not to.

Note: I do not believe I am in any way responsible for the biggest financial scam in history. Madoff was a lying, cheating thief, and the fraud he perpetrated has nothing at all to do with me, my father, or any of my beliefs. But the way I was taken in, my eagerness to give financial responsibility over to yet another powerful man, my willingness to surrender all of my money to an investment I didn't understand, and my lack of connection with money—the expression of my own hard work—have nothing to do with Bernie Madoff.

There is a choice to be made: Continue surrendering power and money into the hands of charismatic, intimidating, powerful-appearing people—and deal with the pain of loss when it doesn't work out—or stop, look, ask questions. Not from blame but from curiosity.

Do we really have to keep repeating the same patterns over and over?

Is money so impossible to understand?

And are our beliefs and feelings about finances so painful that examining them will destroy us?

Really?

One of my students says: "The part of me that never learned to be with uncomfortable feelings is not sure I can bear the raw, gut-wrenching loss of financial status, as well as all the other losses I can't control, that are multiple at the moment. Fears of being homeless lurk in the dark. Fears of gaining my weight back scare me, as I struggle with all the adversity, increasing the urge to use food. And somehow I still can't seem to figure it all out, get it together, with money or food."

Yes, I tell her, being with uncomfortable feelings is uncomfortable, but so is being a victim of a scam. Losing your financial status is painful, but so is acting as if you haven't lost it and running up credit-card debt. Not eating when you're not hungry is hard, but so is judging and shaming yourself when you binge. Getting it together means letting it fall apart.

It's not, as I tell my retreat students, as if one way is painful and the other way is filled with fuzzy, romping puppies. Breaking free from compulsive eating takes work, but so does bingeing. Looking at your beliefs about money is infinitely better than continuing to pay 23 percent to Visa every month.

Our ideas of what it will feel like when we actually acknowledge our part in the mess we're in have nothing to do with what it actually feels like when we acknowledge the mess we're in. One of my student writes: "I thought I would always live from cupcake to cupcake, bill to bill. I thought that was the best I could do, that I needed the mindless way I spent money and ate to drown out my fears about the meaninglessness of life. I was scared that there was a black hole that was going to swallow me up when I let go of eating and spending and trying to push myself to be more or different than I was. But what I found was better than I ever imagined: when I stopped running, my stories about what I needed to run from were mostly in my head. Seeing that, and letting myself tell the truth about some of the pain of those old losses, has been like getting a ticket to the present moment—which is so much better than my past."

Based on our lives with adults who were themselves confused about their relationships to money (and who isn't?), we form a set of lopsided and limited beliefs about our financial capacity. Many smart, powerful women become spineless and clueless when faced with making financial decisions. The only way to remedy this situation is to face it directly and to realize that we are running from monsters that don't exist.

11

Women and Money

One woman was the wife of an attorney with a terminal disease. The second was a painter, and the third was a business coach. We were splayed on a couch at a birthday party, eating olives, hummus, and carrot sticks, when the subject of money happened to slip into the conversation. (It wasn't me, I swear.) Abigail, the coach, asked how I was doing since the Madoff loss a year earlier.

"Really well," I said. "We are both still working." And since we were now on my new favorite subject, I said, "What about you? Have people cut back on coaching sessions since the Great Recession?"

"I don't need to work anymore," she said. "I have enough money."

Minnie, the painter said, "Wow! Enough money! I'm not sure I've heard those two words together in a long time." The lawyer's wife, Peach, put down her olives and leaned in closer. "I want to hear what it feels like to have enough money," she said.

"Oh, don't get the wrong idea. It's not that I'm so successful or smart. It's from the settlement I got from the accident."

Five years ago, Abigail was hit by a drunk driver as she bicycled across a Santa Fe street during a vacation. Her hips were crushed, her lungs were punctured; on the way to the hospital, she was dead for two minutes before the paramedics resuscitated her. Five years, six operations, and an excruciating amount of pain later, she can walk again.

I turned to Abigail, who was smoothing out the wrinkles in her ocean blue velvet tunic. "What do you think would have happened if we believed you made the money by investing or having a successful practice?"

A piece of her hair fell in front of her eyes and she pushed it away, curled it behind her left ear. "You might have been threatened or envious, decided I wasn't one of you."

"So it's okay to have money if you get it by almost dying?" I asked.

Before she could answer, Peach said, "I know how she feels. People don't like people with money; it's better, if you have it, to not let anyone know. And it's easier not to think about it at all. Even though my husband has a terminal disease, I have no idea where our money is invested or how to handle our finances when he dies. Whaddya think? Am I resistant or what?"

"Most of my money is in a safe-deposit box in the bank," Minnie said.

Peach gasped, dropped her carrot with hummus on the floor. "Minnie, even I know that that's really dumb. You are not even getting 1.5 percent interest on that money."

"But at least I can sleep at night, knowing it's still there," she said, looking directly at me. "At least no one is using it for some awful Ponzi scheme."

Oy.

Given the fact that I was a recent convert to the need to be fiscally aware and that my economic knowledge was on the scant side, the fact that I seemed to be the financial whiz kid in this group was not exactly good news. Nor was the direction of this conversation. Why hadn't I just kept my mouth shut?

"Great leggings," I said to Abigail, gazing at the tiny silver stars parading up and down her black-clad thighs. "Thanks," she offered. "I got them on sale at Shunzi." I was about to launch into the where'd-you-get-the-tunic topic or begin the "organ recital," as Ram Dass calls the soliloquy of various ailments—anything to alleviate the tension—but then Abigail turned to Minnie and said, "I understand the safe-deposit thing. I used to have money in stocks, but whenever I'd listen to my broker, my head would start feeling heavy and my eyes would get tired and I'd want to get off the phone immediately."

Head nodding and yup-me-too's abounded from the

sisterhood of olive eaters. “I get a headache whenever my husband talks about money,” Peach said.

“It’s just not worth it,” Abigail rejoined.

“I get sick to my stomach when I am at my broker’s office,” Minnie said, “and then I distract myself by wondering what he would be like in bed. Which makes me even sicker!”

“Girls,” I say. “Not understanding where your money is going does not end up well.”

During the dozens of times I asked Richard, the head of our feeder fund, about Madoff’s strategy, my mind began wandering within the first two minutes of his answer. After five minutes of not understanding anything he said, I couldn’t wait for him to shut up. *It’s a guy thing,* I’d say to myself. *If Matt and Richard understand, it must be okay.*

As if.

I ask Abigail if she’s invested the accident settlement. “Yes,” she says, “I’m a partner with someone who takes care of everything. He lends out the money to people who can’t afford to buy mortgages, and we collect interest on the loans. Although we’ve had a few properties foreclosed in the last year, we’re basically doing well.”

“Do you understand how he structures the loans?” I ask.

“No, I don’t really talk to him about it because I don’t understand what he says. I just want him to handle the whole thing. I trust him completely.”

It seems that most women to whom I’ve spoken don’t want to think about money. Even the ones who are smart and successful, relatively sane and grounded. When I start asking money questions, they say, "Gee, I don't know. I've never thought about that" or "I'm not so interested in this whole money arena." Or, "I'm smart, I'm capable, I could understand money if I wanted to, but I just don't want to."

It's as if there were a disconnect in the brain, as if thinking about money—what it means, how to use it, where to put it—were like asking an orchid grower to elaborate on string theory. One of the most painful parts of my financial life that the Madoff mess revealed was my disengagement from the money I made. I didn't know how to connect the work I loved doing with the money I made doing it. I'd give a lecture or present a workshop, get a check, and deposit it in the bank (i.e., my Madoff account), at which point it simply became a number. I believed (without admitting it) that it was the man's job to figure out (and pay for) the living expenses and my job to spend money on all the extras. I saw myself as an updated version of a 1950s housewife who polished the Formica tables, waxed the floors, cooked the dinners, took care of the children so that her important, smart husband could work hard and make the money. Except that we had no children, I didn't cook or do floors, and I worked as hard as Matt did. Still, I was a money fluff.

Soon after we'd lost our savings, Matt and I were shopping at Costco. We loaded our cart with two twenty-five-pound bags of sugar to feed our throngs of hummingbirds, a few bags of avocados, two *huge* bottles of mustard, and a six-dollar container of spreadable goat cheese that would probably cost nine thousand dollars anywhere else. When the cashier started to ring up our purchases, I waited for Matt to reach in his pocket, pull out his wallet. "Didn't you bring your wallet?" he asked when he saw that my hand was not making a dash for cash.

"No," I said, "I forgot."

"Again?" he asked. "Are you and your money stuck together with Velcro? Have you noticed that no matter how many times we talk about bringing your wallet to Costco, you keep forgetting?"

I had noticed, but I didn't want to let him know that I'd noticed. I wanted him to think that, oops, it was an accident. I just happened to forget my money. Again. But here's what I actually believed: Matt's money was the real money, the money we used to pay for the things we couldn't live without: our mortgage, electricity, phone bills, house insurance, health insurance, food. My money was the play money, the money we used to pay for things we didn't need but (I believed) I couldn't live without: more clothes, furniture, flowers, skin care, preventive health care, and my assorted pairs of black boots.

The way I saw it, Matt had a serious career as a business speaker and I dabbled here and there, tried my hand at writing. The fact that I'd written eight books or that I'd made as much money as Matt since we'd been together did not penetrate the hermetically sealed vault in my psyche that separated men's money from women's money.

The sad, sorry truth was that when I went shopping with Matt, I didn't take my wallet with me because I didn't believe it was my job. I wanted nothing to do with money except to make it doing what I loved and spend it buying things I didn't need. This included staying ignorant about where we put our investments. And why. Not only was I a firm (but unconscious) adherent to financial gender division, but I also believed that the world of money was so complex and abstract that it was impossible to understand. And I had better things to do with my time.

It was very much like my relationship with food in the early days. I'd see a lemon coconut cake and I'd want to eat it. Or I'd feel lonely or heartbroken and I'd want to binge. The food I ate had no connection to the body receiving it; real issues like getting enough protein to sustain my energy or enough calcium to strengthen my bones were irrelevant. The path and function of food after it left my mouth had nothing to do with me; like the famous Mr. Duffy in James Joyce's *Dubliners*, I lived a short distance from my body. Since my way back to food sanity was not through judgment or shame, I know that the way back to financial sanity is not by banishing myself to the land of the overprivileged and underliberated and taking Minnie, Peach, and Abigail with me. The first step out of the darkness is to realize that you're in it and to assume that if you refuse to turn on the light, there are exquisitely good reasons.

"So, have you ever asked your friend about the people he loans your money to?" I asked Abigail.

"Only once or twice," she said, "but he tells me that who they are doesn't make much of a difference. All he wants to know is that our loans are secured by the houses."

"So you could be lending money, say, to men who beat their wives?"

Minnie elbowed me in the side and glared. "We're at a party, for God's sake," she whispered.

"You're carrying this too far, Geneen," Abigail said. "First of all, I already told you that I don't know much about what he's doing. Secondly, it's a business, and businesses are all about the bottom line."

Ah, the proverbial bottom line. After I wrote off the possibility of understanding what Richard called "Madoff's split/strike conversion strategy," I filled in the gaps of my understanding with a self-constructed fantasy: Until the day he got arrested, I believed that Bernie Madoff was a close friend of Richard's father's and that together they started a small—very small—investment business that included each of their families and maybe thirty of their closest friends. My fantasy was lovely and utterly wrong. The truth was that even if Madoff had been investing our money rather than using it to buy yachts, watches, and houses for himself, he could have been buying stock in logging companies that stripped Amazonian rain forests or in companies that produced genetically modified seed. Or in a thousand other ventures that went against, and possibly destroyed, what I valued most. But I never carried my thinking that far, and even if I had, I had so distanced myself from what happened to my money after it left my hands—in the name of greed and the bottom line—that I probably wouldn't have done anything differently.

• • • • •

I was in my late thirties when I realized that the way most people made money was by investing what was left after expenses in the stock market or other ventures, not putting it in savings accounts the way I did. When I started talking to people about where and with whom to invest, I quickly discovered that making money from money was a world unto itself, a parallel universe that operated on four rules: Leave your heart at the door, don't think about the little guys, there is never enough, and the bottom line is everything.

Implicit in these fundamentals was the tacit understanding that a person could love his blood family while financially raping everyone else's—and that that kind of coldness was a prerequisite, was in fact worshipped, in making big money. Like the Enron traders in *The Smartest Guys in the Room* who gleefully shout, "Burn, baby, burn," as wildfires leave people dead or homeless—and increase the price of utilities. Or the bankers on Wall Street who invented junk mortgages but didn't consider how they would affect the people who would lose their homes because of them. "The careless people," as F. Scott Fitzgerald wrote, who "smashed up things and creatures and then retreated back into their money."

No one said these things out loud. No one said, "To make real money you must divorce yourself from what you cherish," but it was understood that making money from money had different rules than life itself, mainly doing things you didn't understand or necessarily believe in. And rather than question the heady, well-established world of complex financial instruments and fast-talking brokers (men and women) in beautifully tailored suits, almost everyone to whom I've spoken spaces out, distracts themselves, feels stupid, or otherwise disengages from the connection with the money they make.

Financial adviser Catherine Austin Fitts created an alternative to the Dow Jones Index: the Popsicle Index, which is "the percentage of people [in your community] who believe a child can leave their home, go to the nearest place to buy a popsicle or snack, and come home alone safely."

"The purpose of the Popsicle Index," she writes, "is to inspire conversation about what it means to feel safe and secure where you live and work, to be physically free to wander without concern and to identify and shift the people and things that contribute to or drain that feeling."

According to Fitts, "It is clear that the drain we are experiencing is spiritual, legal and financial—and that our economy is . . . organized around the Dow Jones going up while the Popsicle Index is going down."

We live with a sense of doom and the awareness that the world as we know it is falling apart. We can't eat fish (the ones that are still alive) from the oceans because they're poisoned with mercury; we can't drink water from rivers and reservoirs (the ones that haven't dried up) because they're polluted with chemicals; we can't eat vegetables from farms (the ones that are still in business) because they're sprayed with pesticides. And we're afraid to leave our children alone for five minutes in a supermarket or shopping mall. But connecting that feeling of doom with the same dollar bills we use to pay for rent and gas and milk—or about which we listen to our accountant or broker—is as hard to comprehend as buying insurance for a subprime mortgage diced and sold in dozens of pieces—and for which no actual money was ever exchanged. The world of finance is so removed from anything real or relatable—so "over there"—that we can't find a place for ourselves within it. But because we live in a world where money is used as a medium of exchange, we need to consider what to do with it, how to spend, give, and save it. When that very process gives us a headache, it's easier to give the responsibility to someone else.

For most of my years as a compulsive eater, I wanted someone else to tell me what when and how much to eat; I wanted rules to follow, instructions to obey. I felt so out of control, so overwhelmed by the sheer number of choices, and so desperate to lose weight that the thought of shouldering the responsibility and trusting myself with food felt, as I've written before, like handing an ax to an ax murderer.

Which is basically the way I felt about the money I made. I've spent most of my adult life engaged in, and passionate about, understanding the addictive relationship to food and using it as a transformational path. I've put in decades of what Austin Fitts calls "living equity"; I've crawled back from the verge of suicide, spent countless hours in therapy, spiritual practice, and at my desk following the relationship with food, as Shunryu Suzuki-roshi says, all the way to the end. It's been my passion, my deep love, my life's work. And yet the energy

I received in exchange for that passion—aka money—I surrendered to people whose values I didn't share and investments I didn't understand. And that was the acceptable way, the way that everyone I knew did it. When I asked a Madoff investor who was a friend of a friend why she invested her retirement savings in a feeder fund, she said, "I asked around; I saw what the rich guys were doing and I figured that they had the answer. I figured that all of them had a Madoff in their lives; I wanted to be like them, make my money work for me, do it the smart way. Now I've lost twenty years of hard-work money—and I'll never get those years back."

Money is expensive—we pay for it with moments that will never come again—and then we toss those moments away as if they have nothing to do with us. As if there were no connection between the numbers in our bank accounts or retirement funds and the hours of our lives we spent training, struggling, commuting, at our desks and away from our families. Even Abigail—especially Abigail—who paid for her money with five years of her life and countless hours of rehab and pain—flicks her money away as if what happens to it after it leaves her hands has no relation to what it cost her to have it.

Money has become so charged with meaning and, at the same time, so removed from our day-to-day lives that we've forgotten what it actually is: something we made up. Money doesn't exist in nature. It doesn't grow on trees. It doesn't fly in windows or walk out doors. We print and manufacture it so that exchanges are convenient. Instead of bartering cows or shells or stones, we use pieces of paper that have no more inherent meaning than a piece of crumpled newspaper. And the problem is that what we created to make our lives easier now enslaves us, controls us, determines our worth or lack of it. We've forgotten that it's just a stand-in, a vehicle, a representation that *we made up;* we feel so controlled by money, so at its mercy, and so befuddled about how to repair the situation that after the tangibles are covered (and sometimes before), we surrender responsibility for it.

But when we disavow the money we make, when we don't understand where it is going or what we are supporting with it, when we say we don't have time or it gives us a headache or it's someone else's job, we disavow what it takes to make that money—our time, our energy, our values, *our lives.*

And if the first step of getting out of the darkness is to realize we're in it, it's helpful to tell ourselves the truth about our situations. Because, as I often tell my students, if you're looking at a map of where you want to go but you have no idea where you are beginning from, there's no way to proceed. And although for the moment most of us aren't even standing—we're crawling around on all fours groping in financial darkness—it's important to remember what Buddhist teacher Stephen Levine said: The only people he knows that have their shit together are standing in it at the time.

When I feel overwhelmed with my financial ignorance or greed, I keep going back to how I worked my way out of the food addiction: with infinite compassion, curiosity, and acceptance. By understanding the exquisitely good reasons I started overeating to begin with—which, though many, boiled down to the imperative to survive and the belief that I had no other choice but turning to food.

For me, chocolate and ice cream were lifesavers. They didn't talk back or hit or leave; I used them to comfort me because no other comfort was available. When I saw that I did my best, I could release myself from the shame, punishment, and self-loathing—and it was only then that I could begin to deeply understand and change my relationship with food.

Although my relationship with money is still fraught and distorted and littered with disastrous decisions born of greed and ignorance, I know that if I start calling myself names, if I start psychologically cutting myself and smashing myself against walls, I'll be a bruised, smashed person who is also greedy and ignorant.

We all have insane relationships with money; we come from a culture in which money is worshipped, in which, as author Lynne Twist writes, our three money mantras are "There's not enough," "More is better," and "That's just the way it is" (and there's no point in trying to change). After successfully dealing with my own food addiction and spending thirty years working with what to others seemed too painful to resolve, I know that no matter how unconscious or distorted, no matter how hopeless or painful a situation may appear, there is always a way through. Every single time.

Here's the real bottom line: The only people who don't

have insane relationships with money are those who were willing to examine their insane relationships with money.

I believe that our relationship with food is a perfect mirror for every belief we have about being alive. And so, it seems, is the relationship with money. Because it only has the meaning we give to it, the way we think about and spend money reflects what we believe about abundance, deprivation, scarcity, and worth. Do you hoard? Do you binge? Do you believe, as one of my students says, that you're alone in a hostile universe and that day-to-day life is an endless shlep of you against the world? Or that there's not enough to go around and unless you take more than your share you'll end up with nothing? According to Lynne Twist, "If you want a clear picture of your priorities in life, who you are, and what you care about, look at your checkbook, your credit-card bills, and your bank statement. The way money flows to you and through you to other purposes isn't unrelated to your life."

Before you change your actual behavior, you need to understand what's driving it; if you don't, no matter how many noble resolutions you make, you will soon revert to behaving in accordance with your deepest beliefs. Everyone does.

When I interviewed Fitts, she said, "There are wonderful, good-hearted people who don't realize that they are destroying the world by the financial choices they make. Each of us gets a vote; we get to choose what kind of energy we put into the world with each dollar we spend."

She tells a story about being at lunch with three friends.

One of them mentioned that she'd taken out a small business loan for 8 percent at Citibank. The second one had a Citibank Visa card and was paying 23 percent on her debt. The third had a CD with the same bank and was getting 2 percent on her money. Fitts said that it suddenly occurred to the one with the CD that Citibank was loaning her friends money at a high rate but that she was loaning Citibank money at a ridiculously low rate. Over Caesar salads and amid talk of politics, energy conservation, and eyeliner, the woman with the CD realized she could loan her two friends money at a lower rate than they were getting from the bank but a higher rate than the bank was offering her. "And while loaning money to friends has its own issues that need to be worked out at the very beginning," Fitts said, "it's a lovely way to use your resources to benefit the people you love. In that way you increase real wealth."

I tell this story to the three olive and hummus eaters at the party. Abigail says, "I never, not once, considered what having money cost me—I didn't *want* to think about how I got it or where I funneled it."

Minnie says, "It is mind-boggling to imagine a world in which people are actually conscious about money. It seems as if everything would change, because if businesses that thrive are the ones that get the most money, then think about what could happen if we redirected the money flow. . . ."

Peach says, "You girls have stars in your eyes. This whole financial consciousness thing sounds hard; I'm still not convinced of the benefits. And even if *we* change, there's the rest of the money-grubbing culture. But I'm willing to start. I'm willing to see."

Last week (and three weeks before that) I brought my wallet to Costco (it's my new favorite place, a GOM, as I say to Matt—Gift of Madoff) and paid for yet more sugar for our hummingpigs, enough toilet paper to stock a small city, and two jars of neck cream that promised to keep the lines under my chin from multiplying. I often tell my students that if one person can change, anyone can change. If one person can wake up to the basic kindness of her true nature, it's possible for all of us to wake up. If Ms. Velcro fingers can bring her wallet to Costco, there is, I am certain, hope for the human race.

EPILOGUE

What Was Found

It's been a year and a half since we lost our money, and we've had a rather large and equally stunning reversal of fortune. My book *Women Food and God* has been on the *New York Times* best-seller list for fourteen weeks, and although I won't get the money from those sales for another year, the royalty check will be substantial. My retreats are filling up quickly, my workshops are packed, and there is standing room only at my book readings. Everything I lost is coming back. I feel unspeakably fortunate and somewhat astonished at this turn of the wheel; it happened very fast, and I'm not sure how to absorb the information, what to do with it. It's as if it were happening to someone else, as if I were watching a movie called *Losing Everything and Getting It Back* and wondering how the once-broke, now-best-selling author feels—because she's not letting on.

In Daniel Gilbert's book *Stumbling on Happiness*, he wrote that people are terrible predictors of what will make them happy. We think being rich or going to Tahiti or having a gaggle of kids will be the answer, but we are consistently wrong. "Indeed," he writes, "an act of parenting makes most people about as happy as an act of housework." And in a study done at the University of Liège, psychologists discovered that the "wealth condition—i.e., having access to the best things in life—may actually undermine one's ability to reap enjoyment from life's small pleasures."

But then again, I already knew that having my pre-Madoff money didn't stop me from obsessing and worrying and convincing myself that no matter what we had, it wasn't enough—and I already knew that losing every penny of it did not make me unalterably miserable. It's not that having money doesn't change things—it does. It gives me choices, allows me to relax about medical care, makes operating in the world so much easier. I can pay off my house, put on a roof that doesn't leak in the winter rains, begin a retirement account—but the changes seem to be on the outside, not on the inside.

· · · · ·

When we lost our life savings, I couldn't believe how blind I had been or that I hadn't paid off my house, put aside funds for family and friends, and given away a quarter of what we had. From the perspective of losing everything, having *anything* seemed like winning the lottery. I decided—made a commitment to myself—that if I ever had money again, I would live with it very differently.

But that was then. In the past month, I've received calls and letters from family members asking for money, and once again I feel like I don't have enough to give away.

Ouch, ouch, ouch.

Having money is sort of like being thin: It's never the way you imagined it would be when you were on the other side. My students who want to lose weight imagine a world of contentment and love and fabulous clothes when at last they lose weight. Then they start losing weight and they get frightened, begin telling me that they are worried that people will have more expectations of them, that they won't have any excuses to feel bad or sad or depressed. That even with just five or ten pounds lost, their friends have begun envying and excluding them. It's not unusual for a person to suddenly find themselves gaining back the weight they lost, and although they feel like a failure again, they have unconsciously decided that they'd rather stay fat than be abandoned.

Although there is a compelling list of reasons to lose weight—health, longevity, attractiveness—there is a much more compelling (and unspoken) list of reasons to keep it on. When a person has to choose between being loved or being thin, she will always, every time, choose being loved. When the pattern is revealed, she explores the feelings and situations that led to her beliefs, and realizes she actually has a choice.

On the financial side, the news abounds with the dark side of being wealthy: Many people who come into a sudden fortune spend their money as if they were in a race to get rid of it. Some end up in jail, addicted to drugs, alienated from their families, or living on the streets.

We live our lives in well-established grooves of identity. We know who we are when we are unloved or poor or fat or rich or wanting what we don't have, and as much as we say we want to change—through big, showy displays of resolutions and pronouncements and regrets—the pressure and familiarity of staying the same almost always wins.

I'll often tell my students that they have to want something more than they want to be thin—they have to want to be close to themselves, to know the truth, to question the very heart of who they take themselves to be—because if they don't, then they will always go back to what they know: their familiar selves, their default ways of operating in the world. Their stories of who did them wrong and what they are owed. The unloved, unwanted me's. The exhausted, overworked me's. It doesn't matter if they are famous and rich and look like they have everything a girl could want or if no one but their own mothers know their names; the process is still the same. Unless we are fully enlightened and illuminated beings (and I've yet to meet one), each one of us is entranced by ways of relating and eating and spending and behaving that are reassuring in their familiarity but do not serve our deepest desire to break free from the stale and repetitive everyday patterns we call our lives.

At crisis times—I call them deathbed moments—being critically ill, being in an accident, being in a natural disaster, losing our money, being with someone we love who is ill or dying—we clearly see the difference between how we want to live and how we are living, between what we value that is priceless and the many ways we've sold our souls, and are willing to do anything to live more authentically. Suffering brings us to our knees, and from that position, we realize that control, power, and recognition aren't doing what we thought they would do: They are not bringing us happiness or intimacy or ease. We decide to turn instead to what we've always longed for—and the only things that will ever satisfy us: contact, love, truth. Then the crisis wears off, and we get back on the horse of more-more-more.

I've had a lot of chances—been a few days away from killing myself and managed to stay alive, lost and gained a thousand pounds, almost died from anaphylactic shock, lived in a wheelchair for two months because of a near-fatal car accident, lost a lot of money, made a lot of money. I've spent decades on a spiritual path, had years of good therapy, been with a loving partner for twenty-five years. Not to mention the privilege of having clean water, enough food, warm clothes, and comfortable shelter. And it's still like chewing nails to be conscious about money—and to use my relationship with it to express what I value most.

· · · · ·

Although I would definitely not encourage anyone to take investment advice from me, I've learned a great deal about the pull to be—and remain—unconscious about money, and about the identities and beliefs we express through our relationship with it. And since this is, after all, the epilogue, it seems fitting to summarize the broad strokes:

It's easy to want to change, but it's hard to actually change. Very, really hard.

You have to be willing to be uncomfortable, enter the unknown, do things your ego doesn't want to do. You have to value being true to what you glimpse as possible—to the heart of your heart—more than you want to be right or get your own way or be comfortable.

And then you have to act on what you discover.

My completely subjective and undoubtedly heretical interpretation of Matthew 22:14—"Many are called but few are chosen"—is that many of us are inspired to change, but few of us are willing to be as uncomfortable as is required to actually change. In the cascade of daily moments when you want to eat or withdraw, when you don't want to think about where your money is going or make financial choices based on your values, where do you turn for refuge? Do you return to the safety of familiar patterns? Do you convince yourself that you have so much to do that taking responsibility for your own choices is too much of a burden? Or do you undertake the time-consuming and intense work of change?

Whether it's the relationship with food or money or drugs or alcohol or shopping, the main factor in any kind of change is whether or not you are willing to truly question your beliefs about yourself and the world. Whether or not you are willing to know the answers. Whether or not you are willing to listen to yourself in a way you've probably never done.

From *Falling into Grace* by Adyashanti: "If someone said to you, 'You can stop suffering. You can really stop suffering completely, right here and right now. All you have to do is give up . . . your opinions, your beliefs . . . and you can be completely happy, free of suffering, forever, ...' For most people, this would be an unacceptable bargain . . . because if we are not willing to find out that what we believe isn't really the truth . . . there's no way we can find our way out of suffering."

And although the topic here is money, it really is—and has always been—the way we use anything, including money, to either increase or decrease our consciousness about our lives here on earth. We can either dig deeper into our well-established ways of seeing ourselves and the world or we can break the trance of the past and question—and take action about—what is true for us now, today.

In the beginning, seeing the truth can make us want to jump out of our skin. It's unsettling to see how we eat and spend or ignore our finances and our bodies. It's humbling and humiliating to see that we value being unconscious or being right more than we value a fundamental ease of being—and that we are paying the cost in the daily discomfort we feel in our lives. But the deeper cost is that by not examining the beliefs that hold our identity together, we are not taking our place inside ourselves or in the world; if we are keeping ourselves overweight to avoid being envied or spending money in ways that are unconscious and do not match what we truly value, we pay in pounds of our souls.

• • • • •

On New Year's Eve in 2008—three weeks after we lost our money—six of us Madoff people gathered at Taj's house for dinner. As we were sitting around the table close to midnight, someone asked the question: If you could have your money back right now, but it would mean giving up what you have learned by losing it, would you take the money or would you take what losing the money has given you?

Matt had just gotten back from Antarctica and was still in financial shock. He said, "I appreciate the question, but I can't even wrap my mind around it. I just want the money back." I wasn't certain about where I stood. I knew that losing our money had cracked me wide open, and I now understood that my relationship with food was an expression of something much deeper than I'd realized—and that I'd been acting it out with money. However, I couldn't honestly say that if someone offered me the money back I would turn it down. But of the other four, each one said that what they were seeing about themselves was incalculable, and they didn't think it would have become apparent without the ground of financial stability being ripped out from underneath them.

Michael said, "I'd started to get complacent. I'd started to loll around in some old patterns, get lazy about spiritual practice. It's as if the muscles of my heart started to atrophy. Now they're awake, alive—and I don't want to go back."

Taj said that the Sufis teach that it's important to learn how to die before you die, and that losing her money was practice for death. Just that afternoon, I had been standing in her living room as she gave away furnishings I had watched her collect over the years: dishes, chairs, vases.

"Isn't this excruciating?" I'd asked as I watched piece after piece get tagged for a friend or consignment store or family member's home.

"It's hard," she'd said, "yes. But it's not as much as I would lose if I was dying. Then I'd lose everything—my friends, my children, my furniture, my clothes, my body, and my life. This is peanuts compared to that. And good practice."

These weren't just empty words. Taj was so broke that she was moving into someone's garage apartment in three weeks; Michael and his wife needed to take in boarders in their home to meet their expenses. Another friend had moved in with one of his children, and his closet was now in cardboard boxes under his bed. Three friends needed to declare bankruptcy and weren't sure where or how they were going to live. Yet another friend had gotten a job as a grocery-store greeter, welcoming people to his local Unity market. Still, it seemed that spirituality was a necessity for each one of them, not a luxury. That in losing everything they had also lost their attachment to who they had thought they were and what they had thought they needed to be happy.

Over the years, I've often asked my students to consider that the very body that they spend hours a day obsessing about will get old, wrinkled, sick, and die—but only if they are lucky. Otherwise, it will die suddenly or slowly and excruciatingly. "But no matter how you die," I say, "you can't take your thinner thighs with you. So make your choices conscious. Decide what you value most. Spend time on that."

From my post-Madoff catbird seat, it occurs to me that spending time perfecting this body is no different from spending time accumulating or worrying about money. No one ever dies rich; they just die.

The poet Rumi wrote that there is a "kiss we want with our whole lives, the touch of spirit on the body / Seawater begs the pearl to break its shell." Sitting with my Madoff friends, I understood that they felt as if what they wanted most of all was that touch of spirit on their bodies—and that losing their money was the seawater. Their values were clear.

As for me, I knew I wanted the kiss Rumi was describing, but I was sort of hoping it could come without the seawater.

• • • • •

In the fourteen weeks that *Women Food and God* had been a best-seller, I'd gone into a whirl of internal dialogue after being asked for money by family members: how I needed to make back what we'd lost, how I couldn't possibly give money away now. Then I began remembering my Madoff-deathbed moment of regretting that I hadn't given more of my money away. And then I seesawed a gazillion times a day: *I should/I shouldn't, I want to/I don't want to, I have to/no one can make me.* Finally, I realized that there was no way that giving my money away was going to feel comfortable if I was looking through the eyes of unlove. When I began feeling compassion for myself as that old identity of unloved and unwanted, I relaxed a little. And then I relaxed a lot. As soon as I related *to* the pain instead of *from* it, I could feel something bigger and kinder than my default identity: awareness itself.

I decided to make an automatic monthly deposit into an account that was only for giving money away: I couldn't make it 25 percent—that was too big a leap for me—but I could automatically deposit 10 percent of what I earned in a savings account and at the end of the month give that money away. I could make a list of people I loved or knew who needed money and companies or organizations that were doing the kind of work that I admired: saving forests, animals, oceans. And I could make the decision to put that money away once instead of agonizing over it every single time I got a solicitation in the mail or heard that a friend or family member needed money.

It's sort of like what I urge students to do when they realize that a particular food makes them sick or spacey or depressed. Although many people interpret the "eat what your body wants" guideline as a free-for-all, it is, most of all, a prompt to take the time to discover what actually feels good in your body—and how you want to feel when you get done eating. If having cheesecake in her refrigerator is too tempting for a student, I encourage her to keep it out of her house. When she feels more confidence in her desire to feel well versus her habitual pull to eat sweets, she can redecide on the cheesecake matter. This way, she makes the decision once, after she realizes that she doesn't like the lethargic, spacey way she feels when she eats cheesecake for breakfast.

Being convinced that no matter what I have it's not enough is my cheesecake these days. When I begin the windup (or grind-down) into Unloved Deprived Me, I catch myself and bring myself back to the present moment, just as I caught myself in those first few weeks of the Madoff debacle when my thoughts threatened to send me off the cliffs of terror and blame and regret. As far as I know, that's the only thing I can do: have compassion for the many ways I am still caught by my past and bring myself back to the present—hundreds of times a day.

The next step is acting on—and taking responsibility for—what I see, feel, know in the present. And this, so far, is what I know and have begun to do:

- remind myself that the way I see things is not the way they are
- secure my basic needs first
- invest only in what I understand

- question those who act like they know what they are doing with money, because even supposedly savvy financial advisers are operating from a belief system that might not match mine. (This also means that I am willing to appear money dumb and frustrate other people who think they are being clear about something I can't understand.)
- be curious about—and actively willing about—deconstructing my beliefs about sufficiency, the need to have more, and what makes me happy
- allow myself to have what I alredy have. Take time with food, people, animals, clothes, trees, eyeglasses
- make money real. Connect what I spend with what I value.
- come out of hiding with Matt; talk to him about every financial decision that I make and that we make together
- come out of hiding, period. Not just about the deficiency and shame, but about the fullness and the moments of contentment as well.
- pay attention to what cannot be measured or counted. Do this many times a day. When I think I've reached the end, begin again.

· · · · ·

When he was four years old, my brother had a dream that there was a lobster in his bed. Even when both my parents heard his screams and ran into his room, turned on the light, tore off the sheets, and looked everywhere in the bed, he wouldn't believe that the lobster was gone. At some point, I padded into his room in my flannel nightgown and joined the lobster hunt. But my brother was so insistent that the lobster was now lurking in a corner ready to tear him apart with its waving pincers that I too started to believe in the existence of the beady-eyed crustacean. "It was here! I know it was here!" he kept saying. My mother and father proceeded to look under the bed and in the closet, in the dresser drawers and behind the curtains. "If it was here, it's now gone," they finally said at the end of an exhaustive search. After peering into every dark area of the room, we all agreed that the lobster was gone—and that it wasn't coming back.

In *The Other Side of Sadness,* Dr. George Bonanno writes, "When my father died, it was as if the house lights had come on. To my surprise, I found that the theater was empty. Not only was I the only one left on the stage, but I was the only person in the entire theater. I had been acting out a play by myself. I could have stopped at any point, but I hadn't known it."

Our lives are like that. We create each part of the dream and then convince ourselves that we're living in a nightmare that's beyond our control.

As I've looked at my beliefs about money in this post-Madoff era, the scary, dark, thudding thing with dollar signs has become fascinating, even thrilling, because it's out in the open. There's nothing I am ashamed of, nothing I won't look at, nothing that has the power to diminish me except the story I am telling myself, the play I am creating in my own mind. Anything anyone can accuse me of with money is undoubtedly true. I've been, and sometimes still am, greedy, tightfisted, afraid, self-indulgent, privileged, unconscious, and blind. But now I know there's no lobster under my bed, and I don't have to be afraid of looking. Money-the-thing—shiny coins or slips of paper—is simply that: a thing with no inherent power of its own. The power I gave to my father and to the list of fancy men was mine; I thought they knew something I didn't. I thought my father's glitter meant that he knew something about money that I would never know. I thought Louis's fast talk was a sign of brilliance. I thought Madoff had a strategy that confused people like me could never figure out. When all the people upon whom you project financial savvy end up in jail, something is a bit off with the projection: the projector herself.

Here's what I've discovered about money: We've already done the projection thing and it hasn't worked. We've laminated wisdom and financial savvy onto people we think have money figured out. Regardless of the kinds of fathers or wage-earning mothers we had—whether they were fast-talking and brilliant or steady or quiet—we looked to them for the template of power and wisdom in relation to money. Because they had all the earning power, we assumed they had all the power.

But it's not too late. It's possible to understand money as an expression of our life's energy and to use it to support life rather than to destroy it.

It's possible to redefine what making a profit actually means and recognize that as long as one person wins and another person loses, no one wins.

It's possible to understand what happens to our money and to use it to reflect what we value most instead of turning it over to questionable characters and complicated investments.

It's possible to find what was never lost to begin with—our ability to feel, give, receive, know, question, learn, change—and to allow that to be the wellspring of our worth. When we spend as much time investing in our inner lives as we do in getting and having more, how we live on this earth and inside our bodies will change.

The Madoffs of the world profit because we let them. They've had their chance. It can be our turn now.

If we take it.

Acknowledgments

After we lost our money, my teacher, Jeanne Hay, and my friends Taj Inayat and Catherine Ingram pointed me back home. For each of them—and the way they grace my life—I am endlessly grateful.

Anne Lamott helped place the *Salon* piece, which was the seed for this book (thank you, Sarah Hepola, my editor at *Salon,* for shaping the piece with such skill). When Annie told me that we could live with her and she would raise us as her own (if I limited my sweater buying to ten dollars apiece), I knew for certain that as long as there was laughter, all was not lost.

My agent, Ned Leavitt, has been my friend, supporter, creative partner, and all-around fabulous person with whom to be riding the waves. What a guy. SallyAnne McCartin was my erstwhile publicist when she sent me an e-mail that said,

"Please write a book about this." I listened to her then—and still do. It is my good fortune to be the recipient of her wicked humor and unerring guidance. My office and retreat managers, Maureen Nemeth and Judy Ross, are daily supports without whom my life would be chaos. Jay Aaron has been both inspiring and touching to work with. Thank you.

Financial experts David Krueger, Catherine Austin Fitts, Spencer Sherman, Lynne Twist, Mark Silver, and Christine Moriarty were willing to spend hours with me as I asked a thousand questions, then asked again. Thank you for your patience and your efforts at explaining what, at first, seemed like Serbo-Croatian.

I also conducted dozens of interviews with Madoff investors, friends, unsuspecting people in grocery store lines, and practically everyone else who blinked at me. Many have asked that I do not name them, but I am grateful to them nonetheless, particularly my retreat students, who are always so generous about exploring their inner lives with me. It is a privilege to be on this journey with you. Menno de Lange, Victoria Young, Blanchefleur Macher, Sarah Fisk, Luke Barber, Howard Roth, and my mother, Ruth Wiggs, were unabashedly honest with me about their relationships with money when I first started writing.

And thank God for the cheering section I call my friends: Roseanne Annoni and Mayuri Onerheim gave me brilliant and considered feedback on the first draft; Kim Rosen, as always, is a fabulous reader and a treasured friend; Lauren

Matthews and Jane Neale, two of my assistant retreat teachers, read many drafts and helped me with the development of the work itself. Allison Post is the schmug of all time. Karen Johnson and the girls meet me exactly where I need to be met. Cheryl Richardson walked into my life and work at just the right time. And Jace Schinderman, my lifelong friend, has read every word in every manuscript I've ever written. It was a lucky day on planet earth when I met each of you.

Last, the people at Viking have been a writer's dream: Carole DeSanti, my editor, immediately recognized the purpose and passion of this subject for me. Clare Ferraro, Chris Russell, Carolyn Coleburn, Shannon Twomey, and the rest of the Viking staff have been unstintingly enthusiastic and supportive during the many steps of turning what begins as a wisp of an idea into a book.

I am awash in gratitude for you and it all.